ENGLISH COUNTRY CRAFTS

SOME BOOKS ON ENGLAND AND ENGLISH CRAFTSMEN

BRITISH ARCHITECTS AND CRAFTSMEN: A Survey of Taste, Design and Style during three Centuries, 1600–1830. By SACHEVERELL SITWELL.

A full and original review of Renaissance building and decorative arts, with 200 Illustrations from Photographs, Drawings and Engravings, including 4 plates in colour. *Medium 8vo* 21s. *net*

THE ENGLISH COUNTRYMAN. By H. J. MASSINGHAM. *Second Edition.*

Mr. Massingham takes six representative types—Peasant, Yeoman, Craftsman, Labourer, Squire and Parson—from their earliest time, and describes their activities and importance. The book is copiously illustrated, and there is a beautiful coloured jacket by Rex Whistler. *Medium 8vo* 16s. *net*

MEN AND THE FIELDS. By ADRIAN BELL. Illustrated by JOHN NASH.

A book about the English countryman, written at first hand. Mr. Bell's nostalgic sketches trace the course of country life and work through the four seasons, and reveal the character, perseverance and humour of the men employed upon the oldest of our industries. The book is beautifully produced, and illustrated by 6 colour lithographs and numerous line drawings by John Nash. *Demy 8vo* 8s. 6d. *net*

ENGLISH CHURCH CRAFTSMANSHIP. By F. H. CROSSLEY, F.S.A.

There is no abler or more understanding guide that Mr. Crossley to the manifold wealth of design, feature, carving and detail in stone, wood, glass, metal and paint, which remains to us in our churches. *Demy 8vo* 10s. 6d. *net*

OLD ENGLISH HOUSEHOLD LIFE. By GERTRUDE JEKYLL and SYDNEY R. JONES. *Second Edition.*

The life of the farm and cottage, its history, amenities and crafts. *Demy 8vo* 10s. 6d. *net*

THE COUNTRYMAN'S ENGLAND. By DOROTHY HARTLEY. With a Foreword by A. G. STREET. *Second Edition.*

The English countryside, grouped under its physical types, and its people—their methods of life, crafts, industries, products and individual ways. *Demy 8vo* 10s. 6d. *net*

Published by
B. T. BATSFORD LTD.
15 North Audley Street, London, W.1

WORSTED WINDER
Circa 1800

(Pyne's *The Costume of Great Britain*)

ENGLISH COUNTRY CRAFTS

*A Survey of their Development
from early times to present day*

by

NORMAN WYMER

*With 149 Illustrations from
Photographs and Drawings*

LONDON
B. T. BATSFORD LTD.
15 NORTH AUDLEY STREET, MAYFAIR W.1

First Published, Spring 1946

MADE AND PRINTED IN GREAT BRITAIN
FOR THE PUBLISHERS, B. T. BATSFORD LTD., LONDON
BY THE WESTERN PRINTING SERVICES LTD., BRISTOL

DEDICATION

To the all too few men and women of England who still prize the standard of their hand-work beyond riches I dedicate this book in the hope that it may help others to gain a greater appreciation of their true values

PREFACE

To write a book on so wide a subject that does not lay itself open to some form of criticism is an impossibility. If one goes too deeply into technicalities there is the risk that many may find it heavy reading; if, on the other hand, one was to ignore them, and paint only a picture of the past history and present setting of the individual crafts, the book would be wholly inadequate. So I have tried to strike the happy medium by giving, in most cases, a brief pen-picture showing the evolution of the craft, together with a very general idea of its purpose and working. The book is not intended for the student, but rather for those who are interested in the life and work of the English countryside, and any who, after reading it, wish to delve more deeply into any one subject should turn to the individual text-books written by the craftsmen themselves.

There is a tendency to regard country crafts as a thing of the past, and to look upon them as a kind of museum piece, surviving solely on the grounds of sentiment. Although many have declined in recent years, such is far from the case, as I hope to show, and to help readers in gaining a greater appreciation of the place each takes in country life I have turned aside from the practice of other writers of dividing up the chapters according to the materials used for the work, and, instead, have placed the crafts together according to the part they play. The fact that many serve several purposes, and would therefore sometimes fit almost as well into other chapters, is an obvious objection to such a classification, but, even so, I feel it should prove the most helpful.

Some may criticise, too, the omission of certain interesting crafts like bell-casting, panel-beating, furriery, leather-painting, bookbinding, and so on. These, and many others, I have left out through lack of space. They are seldom done in the country now, and I intend to include them in a book which I hope to write one day on *English Town Crafts*. I have also ignored all forms of country crafts which I believe to be entirely "dead."

In collecting the material for this book I have visited craftsmen in many parts of England, and have photographed them at work, so that I have been able to study their work first-hand. Nearly every section of this book has been read and approved either by a craftsman or by a responsible rural industries organiser, and any who may think they have discovered an inaccuracy in a description I would ask to remember that craftsmen have their individual methods, and that half a dozen different descriptions may all quite easily be accurate.

A few brief sections have appeared from time to time in articles of mine in *Country Life*, *The Field*, or *The Times Weekly Edition*, and I am grateful to their editors for permission to reprint them.

I am indebted to many people for their several kindnesses and assistance in preparing this volume. First, I must thank Mr. A. T. Moore, Secretary of the Rural Industries Bureau, for his most valued help in so many ways. Then, too, I am most grateful to the following rural industries officials: Messrs. A. H. Griffiths, E. D. Parkhouse, W. H. Hawkins, Rex Gardner, R. W. Baker, H. A. Mabbitt, and Major G. H. Powell-Edwards, M.C. Their kindly assistance, and the useful material which they have given me, have played no small part in enabling me to produce what I hope is a reasonable exposition of a great tradition.

It would, I feel, be invidious to single out individual craftsmen for special mention, so I give them all my grateful thanks and best wishes.

Before closing, I would extend a personal message to Miss Ethel Gerard, head librarian of Worthing, and to my friend, Mr. Hugh Pepper, for so kindly reading much of the book in MS. form and for their many useful suggestions. And last, but by no means least, I am grateful to my publisher, Mr. Harry Batsford, for his advice, guidance and infinite patience.

NORMAN WYMER

WORTHING
January 1946

ACKNOWLEDGMENT

THE publishers have pleasure in recording their thanks to the following photographers for permission to reproduce the following:

Mr. A. H. Griffiths, *Figs.* 67–69; Mr. G. G. Garland, *Figs.* 89, 92, 93; the Publishers of the *Daily Mirror*, *Fig.* 133; Mr. Herbert Felton, *Fig.* 140.

The remaining subjects are from the author's and publishers' collections.

LIST OF AUTHORITIES

MARJORIE and C. H. B. QUENNELL *A History of Everyday Things in England*, vols. 1–4

MARJORIE and C. H. B. QUENNELL *Everyday Life*, vols. 1–4

HARTLEY and ELLIOT *Life and Work of the People*

BATSFORD and FRY *The English Cottage*

GRAHAME CLARK *Prehistoric England*

AGRICULTURAL ECONOMICS RESEARCH INSTITUTE *Rural Industries of England and Wales*, vols. 1–4

ETHEL MAIRET *Hand Weaving*

ERIC BENFIELD *Purbeck Shop*

RURAL INDUSTRIES BUREAU *Rural Industries* (Quarterly Journal)

ELIZABETH HAKE *English Quilting*

THOMAS HIBBEN *The Carpenter's Tool Chest*

OLIVER BRACKETT *Encyclopaedia of English Furniture*

GREEN BROS. (Hailsham) *Spinning Yarns*

CONTENTS

xi

CRAFTSMANSHIP—PAST, PRESENT AND FUTURE

WHILE Adam delved, Eve span. Cain was a builder, and Tubal-Cain "an instructor of every artificer in brass and iron." There were brick-makers who made and fired the materials for the Tower of Babel, and someone must have made the basket in which Moses was found in the bulrushes. St. Paul was a tent-maker, and Simon had a tannery by the seaside. And was not Joseph, the foster-father of Our Lord, a carpenter? Every Hebrew, regardless of class, was a craftsman of some kind who took an infinite pride in his work.

Of all our heritages there is none older or more glorious than the craftsman's, for no one has played a greater part in fashioning the world than he. God made Heaven and Earth, but it was the craftsman, working under Him, who created earthly things. If man had not learnt to use his hands, the world must surely have come to an end as soon as it had begun.

In England we may not always be able to trace our crafts back as far as in the Bible lands, but women were making pottery here as early as 2000 B.C., and possibly even before that.

There were spinners (3, 9) and weavers (8, 11), too, and ropers (20), who spun ropes of grass with which to climb trees. There were boat-builders in England, and coracle-makers in Wales, and tanners (17), who cured the hides of animals in much the same way as Simon. There were carpenters (24) from earliest times, who did every type of wood-work from making the poles for the tent-makers to fashioning crude ploughshares. Flint-knappers had long been established. They were the basis of life before the discovery of metals, for it was they who made the flint tools and implements—hammers, adzes, billhooks, axes, and many others—with which the craftsman worked and with which man tilled the ground and felled his trees. They made also the weapons with which to defend themselves and with which to slaughter animals for food. Without their skill and enterprise, life could hardly have continued. As Dr. Grahame Clark points out in his Heritage volume, *Prehistoric England*, the Brandon knappers must embody a tradition of craftsmanship almost as old as man.

With the Bronze and Iron Ages came the blacksmith (27), who, in addition to working these two metals, also fashioned gold. He had his hammer, anvil, tongs and bellows, and he worked his forge (1) in much the same way as his modern counterpart. Discoveries of parts of waggon wheels and horse bridles show, too, that there must have been wheel-wrights (28, 29) and saddlers (26) in those early days.

Iron was smelted in Sussex and Kent, and there were hand foundries (19, 31) in many parts where molten metals were shaped in moulds as today, the charcoal-burner (34) providing the fuel for smelting. Thatchers (15) and hurdle-makers (37) were in existence, and coopers (2) were busy making wooden tubs about 1000 B.C. There was much quarrying and stonemasonry (4), and copper and tin were mined in Cornwall, and exported to the Continent. Glass (18) was probably not blown until Anglo-Saxon times.

If it is sometimes a little difficult to picture how the prehistoric craftsman worked, the unearthing of early settlements—especially the extremely interesting Glastonbury Lake Village, discovered at the end of last century—has shown that many of these men and women had already reached a remarkable standard of workmanship and skill by the Iron Age. Indeed, it is often hard to realise that their articles were not made by craftsmen of a century or two ago, or even by those of our own time. The discoveries only strengthen the realisation that many of our present-day craftsmen have an ancient and wonderful tradition to uphold —a tradition which we must support and encourage for many reasons— and that, not only are they working on the same *principles* as their primitive ancestors, but often in the same *ways*. These ways may have changed slightly with the progress of civilisation, but the changes have seldom proved revolutionary to the trade.

At Glastonbury the huts—in fact the whole village—were enclosed on the wattle-and-daub principle whereby wattle hurdles were fixed between piles or stakes and daubed with a clay mixture. The huts were thatched, and stone hearths were built. Many interesting relics were found, testifying the age of craftsmanship in England, including a canoe, a millstone, wheels, harness bits, pieces of pottery, spindle whorls, and wooden tubs of a type made by the cooper. The remains of a blast furnace of a kind show that smelting must have taken place there, and there were wooden bowls to indicate that turnery (22, 24) was a practised craft.

Thus, it can be seen that there were established craftsmen of many kinds in our land long before the Coming of Christ, and articles made in England were already beginning to be exported in small quantities.

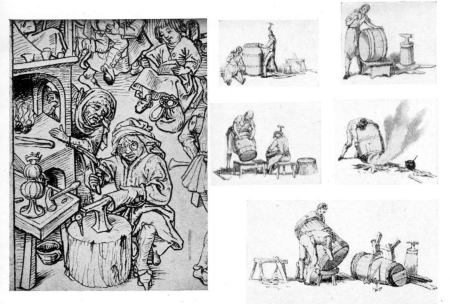

2

3

1. THE SILVERSMITH. 15C. (*The Mediaeval Housebook*)
2. COOPERING. *ca.* 1800. (Pyne's *Microcosm*)
3. SPINNING, CARDING AND WEAVING. 16C. *P. de Galle sc.*

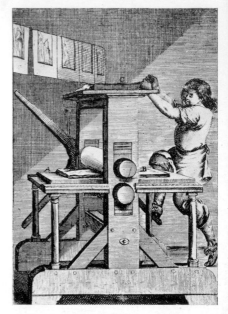

4. THE STONEMASON (Phillip's *Book of Trades*, 1823.)
5. COPPERPLATE ENGRAVING. *W. Faithorne*, 1702
6. A FURRIERS' 16c.
7. MAKING-UP FURS. 16c. *Jost Amman sc.*
8. WEAVING CLOTH

DEVELOPMENT

Discoveries from time to time of new materials widened the scope of work, and the improvement of roads and transport during the Roman occupation caused further developments, as also did the increase in agriculture. With each invasion of our island new forms of culture were introduced, and these gradually showed themselves in the work of our craftsmen, until, by Tudor times, such crafts as pottery (16), weaving (3, 8, 11), cabinet-making, glass-blowing (18), and certain types of masonry (4) had reached a standard of grace and beauty that played an important part in the evolution of art and architecture.

As civilisation spread in England—making rapid strides after the Conquest—the country craftsman lost none of his importance, but rather gained prestige. Every village became a self-contained unit with the blacksmith (27), wheelwright (28, 29), saddler (26), thatcher (15), tanner (17), carpenter, and many others, forming a band of workmen essential to life.

The mason cut the stone (4), or the brick-maker fired the bricks, with which the homes were built, be they castle, manor, or humble cottage. The carpenter saw to the timber framing, and the thatcher (15) covered the roof. While the blacksmith (27) attended to the ironwork, the cabinet maker made the furniture for the home. The linens and other materials were woven in the cottages, and even the candles for the lighting were the product of the local tanner. But not only were the villagers dependent on the craftsmen; the craftsmen relied on each other. How else could the thatcher cover the roof if the wheelwright or carpenter had not first made him a ladder, or how could the carpenter play his part without the blacksmith first forging his hammer?

So it was with agriculture.

In the course of time various districts also became specialised centres for certain crafts, gaining a wide reputation for their work—a reputation which, in many cases, still stands to-day. This centralisation was due, either to the settlement of refugees from other countries in the area, or else to the ample supply of raw material to be found on the spot, which meant that transport had to be provided only for the finished articles— an important factor in days of bad communications. Thus, the Chilterns became the home of the chair "bodgers" (22), who still turn chair legs in the woods; Bedfordshire and Honiton developed into lace centres (21); clay districts gained reputations for pottery-making (16);

Bridport and other Dorset towns became the mecca for rope- and net-makers (20), two crafts which have been carried on in the county at least since the days of King John. There were the Somerset willow growers and basket-makers (36), the Sussex ironworkers (25), and the Burford bell casters (17).

The craftsman not only *lived* in the village; he *was* the village. Life centred round him, and he was often responsible for its independence and prosperity. He took an artist's pride in his work such as can be little understood, I fear, in these days of noise, speed, cheap industrialism, and shoddy workmanship. It is little realised how much we owe him. Besides being the foundation of life within our island, it is he who really started our export trade, thus helping us to become a wealthy nation and a power not to be disregarded by other countries. Long before we could barter with natural elements to any extent, our wool-staplers and spinners and weavers had gained us a world-wide reputation for our wool and cloths, and hides were tanned in English villages and exported some time before the secrets of the craft were learnt in other countries.

Throughout the centuries, from the early days of Neolithic man, craftsmanship in England steadily improved. From humble beginnings some of our country craftsmen have shown, from time to time, such a complete mastery of their subject and materials that they have intro-duced styles that have revolutionised art, and still hold a high value to-day. Chippendale was the son of a joiner on a country estate and Sheraton a cabinet-maker in Durham. To-day, their works remain the pride of art and grace. Wedgwood, too, was a humble rural potter before he set a fashion that was to influence pottery-making throughout the world. And Edney was a Bristol blacksmith before he started making the magnificent wrought-iron work to be found in some of our stately homes.

THE DECLINE

It is a disgrace to our social system and a blot on our internal history that so fine a character as the country craftsman should have been allowed to disappear almost completely with the coming of the machine age.

It was the Industrial Revolution that started the decline, and the decay of agriculture that did its best to complete it. With the introduction of mechanical power in the late 18th and early 19th centuries England went crazy, and, in doing so, lost the glory of her greatest heritage.

9

10

9. SPINNING, BOILING YARN AND REELING, with clock reel

10. BEETLING, SCUTCHING AND HACKLING the flax.
(W. Hincks, *Irish Linen Industry*, 1791)

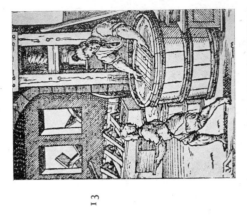

11

12

13

11. THE COTTAGE WEAVER.
(Phillip's *Book of Trades*, 1823)

12. BOOK BINDING, SEWING PRESS AND CUTTING WITH PLOUGH *Jost Amman sc.* 16c.

13. PAPERMAKING.

14. LETTERPRESS PRINTING. 17c. *A. von Werdt sc.*

17. TANNING: soaking and scraping hides. (W. H. Pyne, *Microcosm*, 1800)

16. A POTTERY, with Kilns and Kick-wheel. 16c.

15. THATCHING A BARN. 17c. *H. Bol sc.*

18. GLASS-BLOWING. 16C.

19

20

19. RICHARD TONNOCHY, BELLFOUNDER.
From a 14c. stained glass window in York Minster

20. ROPE-MAKING AND SLEING. 16C.

Articles that it had taken the craftsman days to make singly by hand could now be turned out in large quantities in a fraction of the time by machinery, and at much less cost. Moneyed people invested huge sums in building factories, and their one desire was to produce in ever-increasing quantities. It mattered not that the articles were of inferior quality and design and that they were being further cheapened by their mutiplicity of production. What did matter was that they sold readily, and that the factory owners were therefore able to amass large fortunes which they were careful not to share too liberally with their workers.

How could the country craftsman stand up to this? One by one the old crafts dwindled or died. No longer was it necessary to make everything by hand, from the carpenter's nails to the builder's bricks. The machine could do all that now, and the craftsman might carry on as best he could. The development of cheap foreign imports only helped to speed the decline. Craftsmanship had given place to business; skill and pride of workmanship had been succeeded by ill-controlled mass production. And when even the farmer deserted the friend who had served him so well for centuries the village unit disappeared.

We should not blame the farmer, though, for he, too, suffered lean years. The mechanisation of farming was an obvious advantage, but the lamentable agricultural policy of past governments did not permit progress. The farmer needed to economise, and he could not afford to pay the higher prices to have his waggons made by the wheelwright or to have his implements hand-forged by the blacksmith. He could get machine-made articles now and, even if they did have but half the life of the hand work, they were cheaper to buy. And this was an important factor when so many farmers were faced with possible ruin. Thus, a flourishing national agriculture is as essential to many craftsmen as to the farmer himself. Without it decline is inevitable, as can be seen by the fact that in the first forty years or so of this century the number of blacksmiths, saddlers and wheelwrights decreased by as much as two-thirds, and, until agriculture was revived in the Second Great War, it seemed obvious that there would soon be a further drastic decrease.

SIGNS OF REVIVAL

At long last, however, there is a brighter prospect again. The raising of agriculture from its decaying state has brought more work for the blacksmith (59, 60, 61), wheelwright (62–69), thatcher (75–78), tanner (94–98), and many others. England can no longer afford to ignore the craftsman.

Now that this is realised, we must see that this present revival, brought about by war, is not merely temporary, and that the craftsman is given the chance to regain some of his lost importance now that peace has returned. There is hope that this may come about, for the Ministry of Works and Planning in their Report on Land Utilisation in Rural Areas (the Scott Report) call attention to "the disappearance of the village craftsmen and the serious shortage which has been revealed by urgent war-time needs." What is more encouraging, they call for a revival of country craftsmanship:

It was becoming clear [the report states] that there was not only a demand for the products of actual hand craftsmen as opposed to those of the factory—for example in wrought-iron work or hand-sewn leather goods—but also that there were new possibilities. For instance, if the blacksmith is taught modern methods and provided with modern equipment he can prove invaluable in the maintenance and repair of agricultural implements, as indeed he is doing now under war conditions. . . . Pride in skill and achievement is an estimable trait, and everything possible should be done to provide rural craftsmen with full opportunities to ply their trades. There is likely to be a growing demand for the distinctive hand-made article, especially if it is of good quality and design. Whilst mass-produced goods have enabled the public to acquire many things which otherwise they could not have done, these goods are nevertheless standardised, and this fact ought to stimulate a greater demand for hand-made articles. Rural trades and crafts are essentially part of the old life of the villages and, if they can be made to pay, should continue to be sited in small towns and villages. . . . For all these reasons we recommend that the Women's Institutes, the Rural Industries Bureau, or other appropriate bodies, be afforded adequate resources for the further encouragement of rural crafts and that special attention be paid to the organisation of marketing.

We believe that much can be done to restore a pride in craftsmanship by the revival or creation of guilds of craftsmen and we recommend that the appropriate bodies review the whole question of apprenticeship to such crafts.

Yes, the country craftsman played a big part in helping to win the

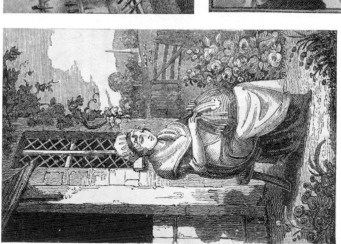

23. Dyeing in the 15c. From Royal MS., 15 E, III, f. 264. *British Museum*

24. The Wood-turner, with treadle lathe. (Phillip's *Book of Trades*, 1823)

21. The Cottage Lacemaker (Phillip's *Book of Trades*, 1823)

22. Turning Chair Legs on a pole-lathe. 17c. *Van Vlie, sc.*

24

22

23

21

25

28-29. WHEELWRIGHTS.
(W. H. Pyne, *Microcosm*, 1800)

27. THE BLACKSMITH
(Phillip's *Book of Trades*, 1823)

26. THE SADDLER

25. A BUSY METALWORKER'S SHOP. 14c. Bodleian MS. 264, *Roman de la Rose*, Oxford

Second Great War, and gave of his best to assist in the campaign to grow more food. As a leading rural industries organiser pointed out to me recently: "The service he has rendered to agriculture is incalculable, and it is only to be hoped that farmers will always remember this by giving smiths the chance to service their machines and by buying the work of craftsmen instead of cheap and inferior machine-made articles which do not really serve them so well in the long run."

How is the revival to be made permanent? Clearly, like the rest of us, the craftsman must move with the times. He must adapt his methods to meet modern needs, and he must be assured economic living conditions at least comparable with those of the town worker. The country craftsman still breathes to-day. Is he to be given the oxygen which will enable his breath to gain strength, or is he to be allowed to snuff out altogether with the return of peace?

A Change of Style

The Rural Industries Bureau, with its county satellites, the Rural Community Councils, are doing a great work in helping to provide the oxygen by training the craftsman to meet modern needs, by providing financial assistance where necessary, by helping him to modernise his workshop with the introduction of a few *light* machine-tools to help with the more irksome and routine parts of his craft, and by teaching him the economic aspect.

At present there are two divergent views among the craftsmen themselves about the use of machine tools. One view is that the introduction of any form of machinery, including even a circular saw, into hand work must, of necessity, lower the standard of craftsmanship. The other is that a *limited* number of such tools are now an economic necessity if the craftsman is to hold his own against the town firm or industrial concern, and that, used sensibly and sparingly, they need not interfere with the standard of work. It is an argument in which I prefer not to take part, for obviously there is a great deal to be said on both sides, and I feel that it is for individual craftsmen to decide which they will do.

Under the scheme of the Rural Industries Bureau, a comprehensive survey is made in every county, under the direction of a rural industries organiser, of local conditions and opportunities. Records are kept, and experts are in touch with the craftsmen in their area to keep them informed of changes and opportunities and to guide them in their problems. Nearly every rural industry is catered for, and the Bureau's staff includes technical advisers, cabinet-makers, potters, textile designers, quilters and many others. There is also a chartered accountant who travels round the British Isles showing the best ways of costing and keeping books—two factors hitherto ignored yet highly important, for if the craftsman is to survive he must be able to make a reasonable living from his work, and not have to do it almost entirely for love as in the past. You cannot raise the standard of his work, but there is plenty of room to improve his status and widen his scope. Thus, free expert advice is given by the Bureau on technical processes to those wishing to include light machine-tools, and help and financial assistance are rendered in the buying of them.

That the country craftsman will regain *all* his lost glory there is no hope. The days when the wheelwright made those graceful waggons as a regular part of his work, or when the saddler did his fine types of saddlery, are gone for ever, I fear.

THE FUTURE

Yet the well-chosen words of the poet, Laurence Binyon, are as apt to-day as when he wrote them at the beginning of the century:

Alas! the fine shapes that marked our old handicrafts have long ago disappeared; the domestic utensils and furniture that gave dignity by their fine simplicity of form and careful workmanship to country cottages have been driven out by dull products of cheapening commerce, things whose making gave no pleasure to those who made them, and whose use gives none to those who use them. Admirable specimens of our old crafts exist, but scattered about, and in remote places for the most part. It is to the old models that those who are now trying to reawaken beauty in the homely arts should turn for guidance. We need not reproduce old forms with servility, but if we wish to preserve an English character, we shall look long and carefully at those works which bring down to us the tradition of those who wrought so well for our ancestors.

There is no place for mere sentiment, however, and the sentimentalists serve no useful purpose. If craftsmanship is to survive, it must do so, not on the grounds of mere beauty or tradition, but on account of its continued usefulness to twentieth-century life. That it is still useful there is no doubt. We may not like mass production—personally

30

31

32

30. HOP-PICKING   31. SMELTING AND CASTING ROUND SHOT
32. A HORSE-DRAWN CIDER-MILL. (W. H. Pyne, *Microcosm*, 1800)

33

34

BREWING 34 CHARCOAL BURNERS MAKING A STACK (W. H. PYNE, *Microcosm*, 1800)

I detest it—but modern conditions make it essential if we are to maintain our place among the great nations of the world and not become
decadent, and if our population is to be allowed to have their fair share
of possessions. The hand craftsman could no longer hope to produce
furniture, wrought-iron work, or any other item in sufficient quantities
to serve the needs of the masses, and even if he could, the cost of living
would inevitably be increased.

Yet in a number of ways he has as important a part to play as ever.
If mass production is essential, every effort must be made to control
the machine and to see that it turns out articles of reasonable quality and
design, and this can only be done by getting the hand worker first to
design and make the article for the machine to copy. He must act as the
brains of the machine if the quality of goods so produced is to be
improved.

Then again, surely even in an age of industrialism, there will always
be a market for the higher-priced goods of the hand worker such a
the machine could never hope to copy. We have not yet reached the
stage when such articles of natural grace and beauty can no longer fit
into the home, and I pray we never shall, for then we shall indeed be
decadent.

There is plenty for the craftsman to do in other ways, too. Besides
tending the farm implements, the blacksmith can make wrought-iron
work for the home in a style really in tone with its architecture, and
the wheelwright will be able to do part-time building and, perhaps,
make tradesmen's vehicles and hand-carts in addition to his farm waggons,
wheelbarrows, trailers, and poultry-houses. The carpenter has little to
fear, and the machine has not yet encroached upon the hurdle-maker.
Thatching is likely to regain some of its lost popularity after the war,
for in at least one county a thatching officer has been appointed to
consider the possibility of developing the thatched roof in post-war
housing, and for improving conditions in the trade generally.

The basket-maker will have more than enough to do unless cheap
German and Dutch imports are allowed to swamp the market again, and,
in spite of machinery, the potter and brick-maker need have little
anxiety, even though they may have to include the making of agricultural drain-pipes to help them along.

In this post-war world, in which it is to be hoped that jerry-built
bungalows—vilest of all desecrations to the countryside—and chromium-
plated furniture will be quickly succeeded by the building of a greater

C

number of houses with grace and dignity and with some pretence to architecture, and by the making of furniture a little more worthy of our great masters, the hand-weaver and cabinet-maker will certainly play an important part.

But if the revival is to be successful, there must be greater encourage-ment for those leaving school to take up hand work; there must be sound apprenticeship schemes with the prospect of a good living wage at the end; and something on the lines of the old system of guilds, which kept men working at a high level, must also be started.

Educational authorities are now attaching greater importance to the subject, and children are being given a better chance to learn weaving, woodwork, pottery, and metalwork. That is a good step. But a school cannot make a craftsman. The best it can hope for is that it may give a child a rural bias, and perhaps bring to light those who may later prove to have craftsmanship in them.

So old and great a heritage can only have its secrets passed on by a craftsman if revival is to be brought about in the right way. The Arts and Crafts movement may have been noble in intention, but it has proved a failure in practice. If more of the followers of William Morris, who started it, had had his knowledge and ability, the movement might have done great work. As it is, too many with little or no real under-standing of the subject took up such work as weaving, and thus gave birth to the "arty-crafty"—one of the greatest enemies of true crafts-manship, and a feature which Morris himself would certainly have condemned.

The whole secret of the craftsman's work is that it combines useful-ness with grace. He never adds weird and meaningless bits and pieces to his work, simply to make it look pretty. He has no time for frills and fancies. The very beauty of his work lies in its simplicity of design and grace of execution, and in such strain must craftsmanship continue.

35

36

37

35. SAWYERS AND THEIR PIT.

36. THE COTTAGE BASKET-MAKER.
(Phillip's *Book of Trades*, 1823)

37. FENCING AN ORCHARD. 16C.
H. Bol, sc.

38-39. FARRIERS SHOEING HORSES.
(W. H. Pyne, *Microcosm*, 1800)

40. FRED EWENS, AGED 96
In his little Saddler's Shop near Chichester

41. THREE GENERATIONS OF THE ETHERIDGE FAMILY
At work at Bishops Waltham, Hampshire

II

THE CRAFTSMAN'S STOCK

WHETHER he be blacksmith or thatcher, woodman or flint-knapper, or whether he makes the tools with which the others work, the craftsman is a character on his own. Born and bred in the heart of Nature, he sees her in all her moods and tenses, and he must work in harmony with her. His materials, for the most part, are her product, and he must work them in the way that Nature will have it. He cannot force the issue. The skep-maker must cut his hazel before the sap runs, or Nature will punish his impatience in his finished article. The thatcher must not hurry his straw, nor the basket-maker his willows, and the spinner must study her sheep.

Since Adam, the craftsman and Nature have moved hand in hand, and it is undoubtedly this nearness to her that has prompted so high a standard of workmanship, combined with natural grace and beauty. From early childhood he has grown to do things in the right and natural way, and he has had no thought but to follow in the steps of his father and grandfather— and probably many generations before them too— into the woods or little family workshop. A woodman's son grows to the feel of the adze almost as soon as to a knife or fork.

To the craftsman, life holds but few mysteries, unless it be the machine, which he has no wish to understand in any case. He has learnt to work with Nature, and, when things go wrong, he will argue that she has an answer to every problem, and, surely enough, he will find it. Thus, he has grown to be independent of things artificial, and is the happier for it. "God gave us hands and feet, and there b'aint nothing we can't do with 'em," one old woodman once pointed out to me. As far as the craftsman is concerned, I often think he was right.

Whatever their calling, country craftsmen have many fine characteristics. Perhaps two of their greatest are their inherent determination always to get the best out of their work, and their wish to continue working to the end of their days, or until their legs can no longer keep their bodies sufficiently upright to enable them to do even the smaller jobs. And some craftsmen reach a remarkable age before they are reduced to that state.

Some Fine Old Characters

Up and down the country men of anything from 80 to close on 100 are to be found still plying their trades as they have done for the last 70 years or more. They may have lost much of their speed, but there is still evidence of their past skill. They go on working simply because they like it. I always remember an old craftsman of 96 when I marvelled at his ability. Looking up from his work, his bewhiskered and heavily lined face smiling genially, he said: "This is my life. Give it up? Why dammit I'd be dead in a week." This remarkable character, who died a year later, still working, had, in fact, retired when he was 80, but with such disastrous consequences to his health that he returned to his job again as soon as he recovered. The mainstay of his life had been taken from him, but when he got it back he was content, and lived and worked happily for a further 17 years.

Perhaps that is the greatest secret of the craftsman—his supreme love of his work. His chief interest lies in finding ways of improving his craft, and, provided he can make sufficient money to allow him to exist, however humbly, he cares little whether his profits will justify those patient hours of work, as so frequently they do not. It is well that he feels so—though he must not be allowed to continue working in such conditions—for otherwise he would have disappeared from the country long ago, and England would have lost for ever a great feature.

In the fields and woodlands and in the little country workshops you will often find one of these real old characters who will have an interesting story to tell you of bygone days. Ask him about his work, and his face will light up with almost youthful pleasure. He will talk as long as you like and sometimes he will display an extraordinary understanding of present-day difficulties and conditions.

In his little saddler's shop near Chichester you may find Fred Ewens (40) still working at 96. Surely he must be the oldest practising saddler in the world, like his father before him who plied the same trade up to his death at 91. Fred's record when I last saw him was sufficient to make even a busy man feel lazy. He told me that it was over 80 years since he started work and that he still put in about 10 or 12 hours a day, "though mark you," he added, "I don't hurry myself these days."

Yet hurry or no hurry, it seemed that he was never idle. After a day at his bench he would be found digging an allotment single-handed to help the food drive. He would never go to bed before midnight, and was up betimes again next morning. A most entertaining character is Fred even though his complete deafness makes conversation, other than by slate and chalk, impossible. I shall never forget him giving me some tips for dealing with a Nazi airman during the 1940 crisis. He had been a crack shot with a rifle and a fine boxer in his younger days. The talk appeared to animate him, for he put down his clam on his bench, got off his stool, and proceeded to skip round his workshop demonstrating—at my expense—the best ways to "get your man." The firmness and control of those punches—despite his 90-odd years—showed me that there was no fumbling either of brain or hands there, and that Fred was probably still capable of a reasonably high standard of craftsmanship.

Abel Peirce, at 95 (62), was another typical of the old stock. He did not retire from wheelwrighting until he was 90—and then, as he told me, only because there was so little work to do and he had two sons in the business with him. When war brought increased work to the agricultural craftsman, however, Abel was ready to return to his old Arundel yard to help out in rush periods. That is a great thing about the craftsman. Let him think that his work is needed and neither age nor weariness will deter him.

Although failing sight forced him to retire shortly before his death, a little while ago, to look at Abel one would never have believed his age. Why, he was riding a bicycle until 4 years ago, and was still a keen gardener! Abel had much to tell of hard times and about work in the old days. He started at £1 a year, and, when he branched off on his own 70 years ago, he constructed his premises where he had worked ever since. From nothing he built up a business that is one of the best of its line in the county.

No less interesting is William Tett, who, despite his 91 years, still wields hammer on anvil, with a skill that would make many a younger man marvel, in the little smithy at Thorverton, a few miles out of Exeter, where he has been working since 1873. When his son was forced to retire recently through ill-health, William refused to give up, and when I last saw him he was busy on agricultural implement repair work. William has almost always worked. He was milking cows when he was 4, while at 9 he was ploughing the Devon fields with oxen. His first job earned him 6d. a week, and he would tell you of the days when he shod horses on a yearly contract of 9s. per horse.

Then there was William Hill (120-122) making bee-skeps in Surrey at the age of 84; and Steve Goodyear working as a thatcher in Hampshire, still thinking nothing of climbing the highest ladder at 81. There is George Rapley, too, making walking-sticks—a highly skilled craft—at 83, while it is not so long since Charlie Green gave up tanning at the age of 94, when the tannery where he worked at Steyning was closed down.

Such men as these make an interesting study in themselves as they typify a bygone age and the spirit of the craftsman of the past. They belong to an age that knew what it was to have to work hard and well for their living, for they are the descendants of those who fought and survived the coming of industrialism and who adopted the slogan that a job that is worth doing at all is worth doing well. If they can pass on no other lesson, and if, in spite of their energy, they are now really "beyond it," they have fine characteristics which many of the younger generation —whose only thought so often is for getting the maximum of pay for the minimum of work—would do well to study if the spirit of craftsmanship is to be revived. And it is to the young men we must turn for the revival.

THE FAMILY TRADITION

But don't let me give the impression that craftsmanship is based on old men. Far from it. While it is true that the majority are either elderly or middle-aged, there are some—though all too few—quite young men who rank among the finest craftsmen of the day, and who are just as capable of good work as their predecessors. They have years of tradition —often stretching into many centuries—behind them, and this tradition has enabled them to maintain the old spirit down to the youngest members of the family. Ask any of them for their earliest recollections of life, and their answer will be connected with their craft or with early work on the farm.

The Etheridge family (41) have been Hampshire wheelwrights and blacksmiths since the reign of Henry VI, and local registers show that they have been working in Bishops Waltham for more than 300 years. They are an excellent example of traditional craftsmen where the spirit and outlook of the younger members are as great as those of the old men I have mentioned. Three generations can be seen working happily together. Frank, the son, has been wheelwrighting since he was 10, while David, the grandson, was only 8 when I saw him at work.

A visit to this forge is an education, for it gives a real insight into the

ki
p
t
t
s
s
T
e
c

42. THE KINNARDS,
    FATHER   AND
    SON: in   the
    Woods   where
    their family have
    worked for 300
    years

43. HAND FOUNDRY:
    A Craftsman making
    Moulds for Agricul-
    tural Implements

THE CRAFTSMAN'S TOOLS

No book on country crafts would be complete without a brief chapter on the tools used by the workers, for, obviously, man must have first learnt to make implements before ever he could start any of his crafts.

To a great extent it is the discovery of these early implements that has enabled archæologists to piece together our prehistory with any degree of accuracy, and the various periods—the Stone, Bronze, and Iron Ages—have been called after the materials which man then used for his tool-making.

The enterprise of the men and women who first lived in England was remarkable. They had few, if any, examples to guide them, and everything they did was in the nature of an experiment. They knew little about anything, and they had to use their initiative or perish. Considering that for thousands of years they were completely uncivilised, and sometimes even numbered cannibals among them, their initiative was often highly praiseworthy.

Thousands of years before metals were ever thought of, man made tools. Mr. Thomas Hibben, in *The Carpenter's Tool Chest*, traces tool-making back 300,000 years to the beginning of the Old Stone Age. Undoubtedly, tools of a kind have been made since Adam, or how else could he have delved? But such ages are too remote for anything more than wild conjecture, and it is not really until the start of the New Stone Age (perhaps 2500 B.C.) that we get any degree of reliable evidence about tool-making. It seems certain, however, that before this period man made great use of pebbles and stones gathered from the stream beds and of the bones of animals. The pebbles he used as hammers, while he made picks out of the horns of reindeer and shovels from the shoulder-blades of oxen and pigs. He found fragments of flint, and noticed the sharp edges, and thus he began to learn the art of flint-knapping, whereby he could knock off flakes of flint just as he wished and so make sharp-edged tools. From the start he relied simply upon finding some way of making adequate utensils with which to do a job in hand. He made his implements on the spot as he needed them, and though they were serviceable, they were undoubtedly extremely heavy and crude.

THE CRAFTSMAN'S TOOLS

No book on country crafts would be complete without a brief chapter on the tools used by the workers, for, obviously, man must have first learnt to make implements before ever he could start any of his crafts.

To a great extent it is the discovery of these early implements that has enabled archæologists to piece together our prehistory with any degree of accuracy, and the various periods—the Stone, Bronze, and Iron Ages—have been called after the materials which man then used for his tool-making.

The enterprise of the men and women who first lived in England was remarkable. They had few, if any, examples to guide them, and everything they did was in the nature of an experiment. They knew little about anything, and they had to use their initiative or perish. Considering that for thousands of years they were completely uncivilised, and sometimes even numbered cannibals among them, their initiative was often highly praiseworthy.

Thousands of years before metals were ever thought of, man made tools. Mr. Thomas Hibben, in *The Carpenter's Tool Chest*, traces tool-making back 300,000 years to the beginning of the Old Stone Age. Undoubtedly, tools of a kind have been made since Adam, or how else could he have delved? But such ages are too remote for anything more than wild conjecture, and it is not really until the start of the New Stone Age (perhaps 2500 B.C.) that we get any degree of reliable evidence about tool-making. It seems certain, however, that before this period man made great use of pebbles and stones gathered from the stream beds and of the bones of animals. The pebbles he used as hammers, while he made picks out of the horns of reindeer and shovels from the shoulder-blades of oxen and pigs. He found fragments of flint, and noticed the sharp edges, and thus he began to learn the art of flint-knapping, whereby he could knock off flakes of flint just as he wished and so make sharp-edged tools. From the start he relied simply upon finding some way of making adequate utensils with which to do a job in hand. He made his implements on the spot as he needed them, and though they were serviceable, they were undoubtedly extremely heavy and crude.

kindly nature of the craftsman, and shows that the old outlook that prompted good workmanship in the past, and which is so necessary for the future, *can* still be passed on to youth. For generations it has been the practice of this family to allow the younger members into the workshop almost as soon as they can toddle, and to let them try their hand at some of the simple jobs immediately they show the first inclination. Thus David already has his own small anvil and tools, and his father and grandfather are sparing no efforts to mould him into a craftsman worthy of their ancestors. Even at this tender age he can do simple forging jobs such as the making of hooks and, when his work is up to standard, he is allowed to sell it. In this way he is being taught to take a pride in his job from the start.

Thus is the true craftsman made. Born and bred in the atmosphere with long tradition behind him, he acquires, rather than learns, craftsmanship. His work comes naturally to him from childhood, and is therefore good.

There are others like the Etheridges, as, for instance, the Kinnards (42), who have been making hurdles in the same south-country woods since the days of Charles II. Son has followed father for generations, and in the midst of their woods is set the little church where, for centuries, members of the family have been christened, married, and buried. They can see it as they work, and it doubtless serves as an inspiration to them. I have watched Fred and his father at work many a time, and have always been struck by the way neither will ever allow even the smallest mistake to pass, even though it may not be visible and may not really spoil the finished article. It is this very honesty that has done so much to maintain a high standard of workmanship in the past. You will find it time and again where there is a family tradition to uphold.

If country industries are to be revived on any scale, more young men will be needed to enter the various trades. To them the work will be new, but if they are to achieve the same high standard, they will need to capture something of the old spirit, however hard this may prove.

44. EDGE TOOL MAK-
INGS: Heating the
Metal in a Special
Forge

45. EDGE TOOL MAK-
ING: Beating Out
the Metal by Hand
Operated Drop
Hammer

42. THE KINNARDS,
FATHER AND
SON: in the
Woods where
their family have
worked for 300
years

43. HAND FOUNDRY:
A Craftsman making
Moulds for Agricul-
tural Implements

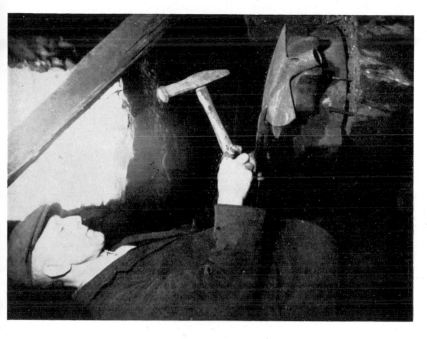

47. EDGE TOOL MAKING:
Beating out Shovels by hand on Special
Shaped Anvils

46. EDGE TOOL MAKING:
Grinding a Bill Hook

48. POTTERY: Getting the Height of a Pot

49. POTTERY: Starting a Bowl

By the New Stone Age, however, men were getting better shapes, and tool-making was becoming a highly skilled craft in itself. Flint-knapping was now widely practised, and man began to find that he could make almost any kind of tool he needed out of this material, although he still made considerable use of bones, horn, ivory and shell.

Tool-makers now formed their own camps. Using their antler picks and bone shovels, they excavated flint mines and fashioned implements for other craftsmen and for land-workers on a barter system. They learnt to grind their flint by rubbing stones or rock against the edges, and to polish it by friction. Thus they could fashion tools of all shapes and sizes with keenly sharp edges. They made arrow-heads for the hunting of animals to provide, not only food, but also skins for the people to wear. They made sickles for reaping the corn; polished knives for sundry uses; axes or celts and adzes for the woodmen. They made curved scrapers for the tanner to use when removing the fatted tissues from the animal hides before curing. They fashioned tools of many kinds—drills, chisels, gouges, and saws—for the carpenter. To make their saws they would take a flat piece of flint, grind and polish up a sharp edge, and cut notches, at the rate of about 27 to the inch, to act as teeth. At first they would make their awls and drills of flint, thorns or bone splinters, binding the top with strips of hide to prevent friction on the hand during use. The carpenter would sit on the ground to work these implements, gripping the object he was making between his knees to act as a vice.

The Neolithic tool-maker further developed his craft by fixing handles to many of his implements, and this was a great advancement, as it meant that craftsmen of all kinds could widen the scope of their work. Obviously, their activities had previously been restricted by the amount of strain that the human hand and arm could stand when the heads of all tools had to be held in the palm. Hammers of many styles—some not so very far removed in shape from those of our own time—were now beginning to be made with handles attached. But the work must have been laborious beyond description. After making the head, the crafts-man would bore a hole in the centre to take the handle, and to do this he had to put sand and water on the spot to be bored, and then patiently twirl and twirl his bone awl, or stick of hard wood, between the palms of his hands until it gradually worked its way through. Sometimes he would twist his awl by means of a thong—holding it in position by gripping a mouthpiece between his teeth—or else he would use a bow-drill, which he could turn by hand. When he had made his hole he would

D

wedge the handle in with fragments of flint or rock. He had other ways of hafting a handle without the tedium of boring. A favourite method was to cut a groove in the head of the tool and then bind moistened strips of hide or damp willows round both head and handle. When the hide or willow dried it contracted and held the whole rigid. Sometimes he would use whalebone to form a one-piece handle and binding. One end of the bone would be moistened to make it pliable, and then tied round the head. This, too, contracted on drying to make a firm binding.

He was now making a larger number of tools, and examples of many of them have been unearthed from time to time in various parts of the country, and some are now to be seen in the British Museum and in local museums near the sites of these early workers. Usually their edges have been found to be remarkably sharp and many reveal a wonderful standard of craftsmanship. There is little doubt that they must have served their purposes extremely efficiently. The similarity in their shape and form to some of our present-day steel tools is often most noticeable, thus proving that these early flint-workers were the original brains of the tool-makers, in that it was they who designed the shapes and styles on which the metal-workers of succeeding centuries based their ideas. They it was, too, who worked out what tools would serve the various craftsmen best.

In a few parts of the country the sites of their camps can still be seen. Perhaps the most notable are Grimes Graves in Norfolk—not far from the spot where their last descendants still work at Brandon—and Cissbury, on the South Downs overlooking Worthing.

The coming of the Bronze Age has been described by many authorities as the start of civilization in that the use of metals speeded and widened the scope of work, and so enabled the people to settle to a more orderly form of life and to start trade. The change-over from stone to metal, however, was only gradual, and for hundreds of years after the discovery of copper and tin, tools were still made of flint. How man first discovered that he could melt metals over fires, and then harden them into any shape he liked, or how he conceived the idea of mixing copper and tin to make bronze, is not known. Mr. Hibben puts forward the feasible suggestion that he probably picked up pieces of what he imagined to be stone or rock, and built himself a hearth, only to find that when he fanned up a fierce fire the "stones" melted, hardening again into a different shape as they got cold. At any rate, it is known that the Bronze Age workers learnt the art of smelting their ore with charcoal, and that they also made moulds of flint or limestone and cut cores. By means of these they made most of the Stone Age tools in a fraction of the time, while also gaining more regular shapes. The nature of their metal made casting comparatively easy, and the Bronze Age craftsmen fashioned beautiful, if heavy, tools.

The discovery of iron set a new problem. Cast-iron was found to be too brittle for the average tool, and so began the making of wrought-iron articles. And here we meet the forefather of the modern black-smith (27) for the first time. By heating up bars of iron until they were soft and easily workable, he hammered out his metal on his anvil, and made most of the tools such as are used by craftsmen now, basing his designs on the examples of the flint and bronze workers.

With the coming of the Romans many new kinds of implements were made. Bronze was used in conjunction with iron for the making of sharp-edged tools, and all were made lighter and less cumbersome than they had been when cast in the soft bronze alone. Then the carpenters' saw-pit (35) was introduced, and soon came the draw-knife—still so popular with country craftsmen—and the plane, and later the brace-and-bit and the circular saw. Steel of a kind had already been introduced for certain tools, but it had been found too difficult to work by hand and so did not come into fashion for tool-making until many centuries later.

Throughout the centuries few of the craftsman's heavier types of tool have altered to any great extent. In course of time they have become lighter, and greater attention has been paid to balance by the introduction of the curved handle for such as the axe. Right down to the Machine Age and the development of steel, tools were forged by blacksmiths (27) or cast in moulds in the small hand foundries. It was a case of one craftsman making the wherewithal for the other crafts-men to work. Individual workmen had their own ideas and needs, and so got the blacksmith to forge tools to their special requirements and designs. Others, then seeing them in use, also had similar articles—with perhaps still further modifications—specially made for them. Settlers from other countries, too, introduced new forms of the basic implements. And so, from the original tools of the Stone Age scores of others have evolved, many serving a similar purpose, but each differing slightly from the rest.

The craftsman's tools have now become so wide and varied that they make an excellent study in themselves for a book, and space will not permit further discussion of them here.

Nearly all tools are machine-produced of steel these days, but there are hand workers—especially woodmen—who still prefer to have their implements hand-made. In just a few—a very few—places edge tool-makers (44-47) are to be found making axes, billhooks, and a number of small tools by hand. They use a special forge for heating their metal which they then beat out by drop hammers before hammering by hand on to anvils of varying shapes designed for the particular article in question. They grind down their edges by lying flat on their stomachs on a platform above a power-driven grindstone. Once this was a common way of making tools. Now, I believe, there are only about half a dozen firms of the kind left in the country. There is one near Okehampton, in Devon, and another in Cornwall, and—at any rate until quite recently—a third in Sussex, near Crowborough. There are still one or two small hand foundries where plough-shares and other agricultural implements are made as of old (43). But that is out of the province of the craftsman proper, so let us set off and see with what skill he wields these various implements.

IV

CULTURAL CRAFTS

OUT of the whole wide field of hand work there are three crafts—
pottery, cabinet-making, and weaving—which have probably had a
greater influence on art and architecture throughout the ages than any
others. They are, in effect, cultural crafts.

Examples of early attempts at design—seen on pieces of prehistoric
earthenware dug up from time to time—lead to the belief that quite
possibly patterns were scratched by finger-nail or pieces of twig on to
pottery, while the clay was still wet and plastic, before ever they were
drawn by charcoal on walls, and that pattern began as a means of
improving the appearance of hand work rather than as a recreation.
Although the perishable nature of cloths and wood has left us with but
few examples of really early weaving or cabinet-making, it is likely that
some form of design—if only amounting to the introduction of a few
odd lines—was introduced at the start of each of these crafts too.

But it is not so much the ways in which the various articles were
decorated as their very composition that has made the crafts influential.
Potters, weavers, and cabinet-makers have had to keep abreast of fashion,
and to work in harmony with architects and builders, each studying the
work of the rest and forming a close liaison between them. The result—
at any rate until the Victoria era—was well-designed homes, artistically
furnished and decorated. Although it is now often difficult for a craftsman worthy of the name to keep in tone with the modern builder without lowering the standard of his work, that liaison does still exist in the
case of our better-class homes, built to the designs of good architects.

POTTERY

We, who to-day enjoy our meals well cooked, owe much to the
hand-potters of the Stone and Bronze Ages. They it was who first made
civilized methods of cooking possible by fashioning—however crudely—
vessels which would withstand the heat of fire, and enabled families to
eat cooked food other than animals roasted over open fires or in pits
as hitherto.

21

It is probably true to say that the advent of pottery was in reality the first sign of anything approaching civilisation or culture—however distant—in this country, as not only did the potter bring in a sound foundation for art by his introduction of pattern, but he also helped to improve living conditions to a very considerable degree. Through him many types of dishes could now be cooked; food and drink could be stored as never before; jugs, spoons, and various domestic utensils were able to be made; and there were many other uses to which his work could be put. Even methods of burial were improved by the introduction of the cinerary urn, samples of which are still unearthed from time to time.

Although many materials have taken the place of earthenware in the centuries that have followed, it was the potter who first took the housewife out of her primitive "roasts" and put her on the path to present-day cookery. Even the aluminium saucepan, so eagerly snapped up in that fateful summer of 1940 to turn into aeroplanes, is really only a glorified form of the Stone Age pot, while the double saucepan dates from the later practice of warming-up milk, stews, and other foods in pitchers or vessels in the ever-hot oven.

Although the early work was naturally crude, as judged by present-day standards, there was a great deal that was artistic about it, while the men and women who did it must have been good masters of their materials.

The prehistoric potter had only his hands and, perhaps, a piece of shell or the broken bone of an animal with which to work. There were no wheels on which to turn the pots—they did not come in until later—and no kilns in which to bake them. Yet, he turned out many serviceable articles with infinite skill. He prepared his clay by puddling it with his hands or feet and, in the absence of a wheel, turned his pots by rotating the balls of clay on piles of leaves. He fired them by placing them on stones and lighting bonfires all round and over them. As the methods of heating count for much in pottery, he must have developed a pretty sound control over his fires, and devised some way of increasing and decreasing their tempo evenly. That his work was of a high standard can be seen by the excellent condition of the pottery that is excavated periodically.

Throughout prehistoric times pottery showed a steady evolution. A crude form of turntable was devised—probably by the Romans—for rotating the pot and, by the time of the Conquest, the potter had not

50. POTTERY:
Making the Ridges on Decorative Ware

51. A POTTER WORKING FOR THE FOOD FRONT:
Mr. W. B. Hunt of Arundel, Sussex, whose family have been
at the Craft for 200 years

53. WEAVING:
Spinning by means of a Spindle much the same

52. POTTERY:
Taking Pots from a Kiln after firing

only widened his scope but had also developed the artistic side. Unfortunately, however, work in other, and more durable, materials —wood, leather, horn, bronze, and rough iron—was developing too, and gradually took precedence over the rather under-fired pottery, so that in the 16th century we find craftsmen still working in a style that had shown but little progress (16). The potter had to wait until the following century for the development of a kiln capable of higher temperatures, which would enable him to bake his ware into a harder substance, before he could compete against this competition.

True, he had his wheel by now, but what a wheel! It comprised a kind of inverted cage with vertical bars. The potter turned it by kicking his heels against the bars to set it revolving for a round or two. As it slackened speed he would give another kick, and so on. Many south-country craftsmen still use a method which must surely be a direct descendant. A heavy wheel, connected to the throwing wheel by a vertical rod, is kicked round by the right foot (16). The early kiln consisted of a perforated stone platform with low walls on three sides, and under this faggots were kindled, the firing being done in the open.

Wherever there were clay beds there were village potteries, and in these little country worksheds all types of utensils, from flower-pots to bread-pans and milk-jugs, were fashioned with great skill. But it was not until the 18th century, when Josiah Wedgwood, who came of a long line of peasant potters, decided to place the craft on a higher level, that the work really started its ascendancy.

Unlike his predecessors, Wedgwood had great foresight and a keen business mind. So (after an unsuccessful partnership which was soon dissolved) together with Thomas Whieldon—undoubtedly a greater artist than himself—Wedgwood carried out scientific experiments for introducing Ancient Greek and Roman ideas, coupled with Italian and French methods, into English pottery. That his experiments were successful can be seen by the fact that before he was 40 he was to open, in Staffordshire, the first pottery factory in England, and was to follow it a year later with extensive enamelling workrooms in Chelsea in the charge of the artist, Bentley. Pottery was becoming the universal ware of every home, both large and small, once more. Wedgwood's lead was soon taken up by others, and gradually there developed an English pottery tradition of artistic and technical achievement equalling that of any other country in the world except China, who still stands in a class on her own. Even to-day Wedgwood pottery maintains its popularity in large mansions.

There have been many fine potters to continue this development and artists such as the late G. F. Watts, who established a potters' art guild in the Surrey village of Compton for making pottery in much the same way as the village craftsmen in Italy, have done much to raise the standard of art, until to-day we have such craftsmen as Michael Cardew, Bernard Leach, and W. F. Crittall fashioning ware of a truly high standard.

Although, unhappily, many hand potteries have closed in recent years owing to the development of the factories, there are still to be found a number of interesting small workshops dotted about the countryside. In some of them craftsmen have worked uninterrupted for centuries; in others they are working on sites previously used by prehistoric potters, as at Ilminster, in Somerset, and at Wattisfield, in Suffolk, where men are to be found using the same clay seams as the Romans. At Wattisfield it is believed that the craft has been carried on ever since Roman times, and the kilns of these early craftsmen have been found in adjacent fields.

Almost as old is the hand pottery at Barnstaple where, it is claimed men have fashioned Barum ware for some 1,500 years. At Verwood, in the New Forest, pitchers are still made as in Queen Elizabeth's time, while at Bideford is the little workshop where church tiles were made in the 14th century. There is an interesting old pottery at Winchcombe, in Gloucestershire, once used by Michael Cardew, but now in the capable hands of Ray Finch, and there are others at Poole, home of the famous Poole Pottery, at Honiton and at Hailsham, where the well-known Dicker ware is made. There are a few in the more isolated areas of the north, and in Wales there is the well-known one at Buckley Common in Flintshire and another of equal interest at Penrith.

For the true country-lover I can think of few more fascinating ways of spending an afternoon than in watching one of these country crafts-men at work.

Clays vary with the locality and each clay has to be worked in a slightly different way, which means individuality at once. And where there is such individuality there must surely be an added interest to the work. In Devon and Dorset alone—one of the best clay centres in the country—there are many varieties. There is the rich white clay of the Teign Valley; the red of Torquay; the far deeper red of the Barnstaple district; and there is the blue round Poole, to mention but a few. In other parts there are further colours such as the grey and the biscuit, and I am told that an expert can often tell where a piece of pottery has been made simply by looking at it.

Before the potter can start to make his ware, he must wash his clay free of stones and grit, for these are his worst enemy if he is to make a good-class article. Even the smallest particle of limestone is liable to cause a crack. In some country districts special blungers and pug mills are used to crush the clay into a dense consistent mass, but there are still a few craftsmen who puddle it with their hands and feet in the old way as at Verwood.

When the clay is cleared of grit, it is taken to the potter's shed, where it is weighed and roughly moulded into balls (48–51). The weighing is important, as each ball must comprise just the correct amount of clay to make a pot of a specific size. The potter who has many articles to make in a day, as in the case of the flower-pot-maker (48, 51), will weigh out scores of balls at a time so that when he sits at his wheel he can work without interruption.

What can be more exciting than watching a busy potter turning out pots as fast as he can go unless it be to see the infinite care and patience displayed by a craftsman in fashioning a more artistic type of ware? One minute it is a ball, the next it is a flower-pot. That is literally true, for a potter once told me that it takes him exactly a minute to throw an average-size flower-pot.

He places a ball of clay on his wheel and then rotates it anti-clockwise. As the wheel revolves—often at an incredible speed—the craftsman presses the fingers of his left hand into the middle of the ball, leaving his thumb on the outside. As the wheel turns, the clay gradually rises in the form of a pot, which is shaped by holding a template of metal or slate against the outside with the right hand (48). An indicator, stretching from the side of the bench, shows the correct width and height to which the pot must reach (48).

As each is finished it is removed, flexible as rubber, by passing a wire strand between the bottom of the pot and the top of the wheel, and is placed on a plank ready to be dried and fired.

Flower-pot-making may be the simplest branch of the craft, but it forms the basis of all other circular work. Jugs, pitchers, vases (50), bowls (49), bread-pans, and numerous other articles are all made in the same way fundamentally. Whether he can fashion only the simple flower-pot or whether he can make those extremely attractive shapes seen in the more decorative ware, depends entirely on the temperament of the craftsman and on his degree of skill.

Considerable experience is needed in making handles, for the question of balance when lifting has to be considered. The handle must admit the correct number of fingers necessary to lift the weight of the full vessel; its section must be comfortable to grip; and, after many other practical points are taken into account, it must be made to look artistic and not cumbersome. Always a shrewd eye must watch to see that handle and vessel become one complete form.

But vessels are not the only articles which the potter makes. There are roofing tiles, tiles for interior house decoration, flat dishes for cooking, and so on. Dishes are made by pressing clay either over the outsides or into the insides of moulds, patterns being formed by means of "bats" which make indentations into the clay (50). These indentations are later filled up by pouring in different colours to form extremely bright designs. Similarly, decorative tiles are made by pressing wood blocks against the plastic clay, and then colouring in the same way.

Whether it be pot or dish, pitcher or tile, the ware must now be burned, and this is done in kilns (52), where the heat is gradually increased for hours to temperatures ranging from 1,000 degrees Centigrade to 1,300 degrees Centigrade, and then decreased at a similar rate, according to the nature of the pottery. Great care has to be taken, as uneven or too rapid raising or lowering of the temperature brings disastrous results. Smaller articles are dipped in glaze baths and fired afresh, but the larger ware is glazed and finished in the initial firing.

The hand potter has a definite future before him provided that he does not copy, or compete against, the large firms, and provided that he retains with well developed appreciation the fundamental human qualities to be found in all good hand work. Michael Cardew and Bernard Leach, by producing beautiful ware, have helped to revive the public's appreciation of high-class hand work in recent years and have shown that there is still a certain market for sound workmanship. Let us hope that more will soon gain that same appreciation.

54. WEAVING:
Mrs. Ethel Mairet,
a leading hand
weaver at work

55. WEAVING:
Making a Warp

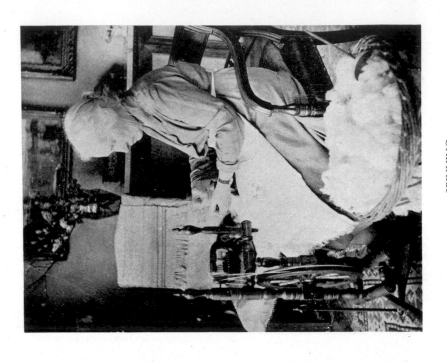

57. SPINNING:
Mrs. May Holding, a leading spinner, at work

56. WEAVING:
Winding up the Bobbins

Spinning and Weaving

The hand weaver and spinner of to-day still spins her wool on the same principles as did the women of the Stone Age, and if the pre-historic spindle (53) is now seldom used, it is only because the 16th-century spinning-wheel (3, 9) is found to be quicker. She cards her wool as of old and dyes it with vegetables and herbs from the woods and garden (23). Fundamentally, her loom has not really changed so greatly either.

Yet she herself has changed. No longer does she spin and weave of dire necessity, knowing that she would have nothing to wear if she did not. Nor does she present the Tudor atmosphere that the modern Press photographer, in search of a "pretty-pretty," would have us believe—sitting on the edge of her garden well, a kerchief on her hair, leisurely spinning her wool as if Time would willingly wait for her. The Machine Age, with the development of the power loom, has altered all that. Although she is still to be found in parts of Scotland and Ireland, the peasant weaver has gone from England and the hand worker survives to-day only because no machine can ever quite obtain that unique quality that always distinguishes hand work from machine-made articles.

Everyday clothing, as woven by the peasant of the past, is now turned out more cheaply and more plentifully by power looms, and the modern weaver must strive for something higher. She must maintain a standard of quality and design beyond the scope of the machine and in keeping with the highest traditions of architecture, dress, and modern living. Her work must always be of use and not merely a thing of beauty, for once use is divorced from beauty it becomes "arty"—a point freely overlooked by so many of the elderly ladies who find weaving a "fascinating hobby" and whose lack of real understanding of the subject often makes their work just tiresome.

The weaver of to-day is becoming a far more scientific craftswoman than her predecessors, and the edge of the garden well is no longer suitable for her. Instead, she prefers well-arranged workshops, sheds, or living-rooms.

Of all crafts, spinning and weaving presents one of the finest examples of the triumph of the hand craftsman in the great battle against the machine (3, 8, 9, 11). With the coming of the Industrial Revolution the craft virtually died out until, as Mrs. Ethel Mairet (54), one of the greatest weavers of the present time, tells us in her book, *Hand Weaving*, there were not more than six hand-loom workshops left in England at the beginning of this century. Yet, although machinery has continued to make great strides, the number of hand workers has risen again until now there are several hundred. No craft has so completely died only to be reborn.

Spinning and weaving is one of our oldest industries, having quite possibly preceded agriculture. Fine cloths are known to have been woven in Egypt before 2000 B.C., and there have been a number of Stone and Bronze Age discoveries, such as the remains of a wooden loom and spindle-whorls at Glastonbury and fragments of linen and woollen fabrics in the East Riding of Yorkshire, to testify its early origin in this country.

Although linen (8) is the first thread known to have been woven, the English weavers (3) gained their world-wide reputation for their woollen cloths. Our climate has always proved particularly suitable for sheep-rearing and in the Middle Ages we accumulated a great wealth from our woollen industry. In their 16th-century volume of the *Life and Work of the People* Miss Hartley and Miss Elliot quote a note from a Russian merchant asking for samples of English weaves as being the finest in the world. We were then the world's principal suppliers, other countries going in more for linen and cotton weaving. Evidence of this prosperity can still be found in the "wool" churches of the Cotswolds, which were built by the wool-staplers.

From earliest times until the late 18th and early 19th centuries the peasant weaver had been a common sight. While the menfolk toiled in the fields and woodlands the women would spin the wool and weave the clothes for the family. The spinning would usually be done by young girls—hence the word "spinster" for unmarried women—and even the humblest cottage home would boast some form of loom. The work was slow, ten spinners being needed for every weaver.

Then came development. The spindle had already given place to the spinning-wheel and now Hargreaves invented the spinning-jenny whereby eight spindles could be worked at a time. Arkwright followed shortly afterwards with his machine, and then came Crompton with his "mule." The loom, too, was speeded up by Kay's fly-shuttle, before the clergyman, Cartwright, with no experience of weaving, introduced the first power loom in 1785, driven by water-wheel. All these inventions did much to stimulate the textile trade, and they were the foundation of the mills of Wales and Lancashire. But they were also the beginning of the end from the hand worker's point of view. Factories soon sprang up with great rapidity, and gradually the peasant spinner and weaver all but disappeared.

It was William Morris—with his remarkable ability for combining art with craftsmanship—and his great friend, Burne-Jones, who really saved hand work from complete extinction. They realised that if hand work was to survive the machine it must have a higher artistic standard. In his workshops at Merton Abbey, Morris combined art and craftsmanship in a way that had never been seen before, spending long hours in research to invent new colours. As Mrs. Mairet points out, his influence was soon to spread throughout Europe. But there was a danger in his work. Most of his followers and imitators were less skilled than he, and lacked the real understanding of their subject. Poor imitations of Morris's work found their way on to the market, and thus his Arts and Crafts movement went awry and menaced, rather than improved, craftsmanship.

Fortunately, however, there have been a few like Morris to continue the struggle. There was Luther Hooper, who introduced Swedish ideas into his design at the turn of the last century, and Ruskin, who tried to improve the standard of work in the Lakelands. To-day we have Mrs. Ethel Mairet (54), who has made a close study of the craft in many lands, Mr. and Mrs. P. S. Beales, the Wiltshire spinners and weavers, Mrs. May Holding (57), whose handbook on dyeing and spinning wool is well known, Miss Grayson, who specialises in ecclesiastical weaving at Clevedon, Miss Kendon of Uckfield, Miss Peacock, and a number of others, all doing much to improve the standard of the craft.

Although spinning and weaving have become highly scientific the work has changed but little fundamentally. The Bronze Age worker made wooden spindles about a foot long with "whorls" to twist them a few inches from the lower end. The spinner held a distaff containing carded wool in her left hand, and attached one end of the wool to the spindle, which she kept twirling by a motion of her right hand. As the spindle twirled she "fed" it by drawing the wool from the distaff with her left hand. Thus the wool turned on itself to make strands or cords. Although the more familiar spinning-wheel, which works on the same principle—that of making the wool turn on itself—is the most used these days, some of the finest craftsmen still adopt the spindle method on occasions (53).

The prehistoric loom is believed to have comprised three poles, one resting horizontally across the tops of two vertical ones, the warps being suspended from the top and held taut by means of weights. The worker stood up to weave and laboriously threaded her strands of wool, known as the weft, alternately over and under the warp threads. The same idea applies to-day, except that a far more advanced loom with a highly developed system of setting it up is now used, while the weft can be passed in a shuttle through as many warp threads as required at a single hrow (54).

The ways and methods of individual craftsmen vary so enormously, and it is now so complex a craft that it is impossible to give anything approaching a complete picture of the work. No two work exactly alike and every design has some individuality. The craftsman must have a wide knowledge, not only of her materials in general but also of the sources of supply in each case. She must know from what variety of sheep the wool she is to work has come, for each variety must be spun in a different way.

When her wool arrives in its natural oily state—straight from the sheep's back—it must be washed and dyed. The dyeing—a fascinating branch of the craft—is a science in itself, requiring much study and practice.

After dyeing, the wool is carded and spun into yarn with which to make the warp (55) and weft. The carding is done by combing out the fibres of the wool lengthways with special combs, known as carders, to render the wool free of tangles, and to ensure that the staple will be used to the best advantage and give the maximum strength when converted into yarn by the spinning-wheel. The speed and rhythm with which the spinner works her wheel has a fascination of its own. Indeed, it has as great a fascination to the spinner, for she will tell you that the rhythm with which she works her foot treadle has an important effect on the finished yarn (57).

When sufficient yarn has been made—and before weaving can start—the warp must be prepared (55). The warp is the name given to the threads which run the full length of the fabric, and which form the base through which the weft will be woven. As the warp may be many yards in length, some means must be devised for obtaining a sufficient number of threads of the correct length, and this is achieved by winding the threads on to a revolving frame, known as a warping-mill (55).

The finished warp is wound on to the back roller or beam of the loom with a sufficient length left free to reach to the front beam. Each thread is then passed through a separate loop, known as a headle, and is attached to the front beam. The warp is now in position and ready for weaving.

The headles containing the warp are suspended from the top of the loom on headle-sticks, which in turn are attached to treadles operated by the feet of the weaver. They are arranged in such a way that by depressing one or other of the levers, individual threads of the warp can be raised or lowered as required, to form a channel through which the shuttle carrying the weft can be thrown (54). After each throw, the weaver pulls forward the arm of the loom to press her weft firmly into place.

By her control of the headles, by varying her colours of both warp and weft, and by a suitable choice of materials, the weaver can vary her work just as much as her skill will allow.

The weaving completed, the cloth is wound off the loom to be washed and shrunk for use.

Cabinet-making

As examples of very early furniture have long ago perished, it is difficult to assess with any accuracy the exact age of cabinet-making. Although it is one of the most superb of all crafts, and one which in many ways has influenced everyday life, architecture, and design even more than the other two, it is doubtful whether it is quite so old. Probably, prehistoric man never thought of making furniture. Everything he did or made was prompted by necessity and, if the idea of furniture ever entered his head, he probably dismissed it as a luxury.

He needed utensils for cooking his food and for holding liquids, so, as we have seen, he made pottery; he must have shelter, too, against the weather, so he learnt to build huts and thatch their roofs. But with furniture it would have been different. What need for a bed when there was always the ground on which to lie, or why make a chair when the bole of a tree would serve as well?

Even as late as the 12th and 13th centuries—when civilisation of a kind had been known in England for some time—furniture was still a rarity. If they had any at all, the middle and lower classes used little more than blocks of wood, roughly hewn by axe and adze from trees and jointed together in the crudest form of carpentry, to serve as stools, benches, and one or two other articles of strict necessity. Even in the mansions and baronial halls, the tables comprised only boards of wood fastened together and laid on trestles, while solid benches of the simplest design formed the main seating arrangement. For a very long time chairs were almost unheard-of—so much so, in fact, that our present-day word "chairman" dates back to the days when no home had more than one chair, and the principal member of the household sat in it. Even so, it was probably a doubtful pleasure, for the few that were made were extremely solid and heavy, and they must have felt very hard!

Chests, which have been made by the cabinet-maker from the start, formed one of the main pieces on account of their manifold uses. Not only did they provide seating accommodation in bed-chamber and dining-hall alike, but they also served as convenient places for storing possessions and as trunks during a move at a time when moves were not infrequent.

But, limited as his scope undoubtedly was, and crude though his style may have been, as judged by later standards, the cabinet-maker was always a skilled craftsman. Even the most primitive chests, roughly hewn out of tree-trunks and carved for decoration, were the work of men with a sound knowledge of their materials and a certain gift for hand work. Yet the *real* cabinet-maker did not appear until Tudor times, and furniture continued to be scarce until the end of the 16th century. A contemporary writer recorded that whenever Queen Elizabeth moved from one palace to another the greater part of her furniture had to go with her owing to the shortage.

But despite the scarcity, in the reigns of both Henry VIII and Elizabeth we find definite signs of progress. The table-trestles were giving place to solid oak legs, fixed to a more substantial kind of top; chests were panelled; a slightly more graceful form of chair now appeared, and in greater numbers; the four-poster bed had arrived; and there is evidence of settles, sideboards, wardrobes, and presses being made for the first time. In each case the standard of workmanship and the magnificence of the carving reveal a greater mastery of the craftsman's tools than had been seen before.

If it produced no sensational changes, the Tudor period certainly showed a sound and steady evolution. Craftsmanship was settling down to an extremely attractive, if somewhat crude, style. The community spirit was to be found in the villages, and builder and cabinet-maker worked in harmony. The builder made his houses low-pitched, solid, and with heavy interior beaming, and the cabinet-maker kept in tone with him. That the result must have been charming can be judged by the all too few examples of Tudor cottages which still stand dotted about the country. If they have not all the labour-saving conveniences of the modern home, who can deny their natural beauty?

In his extremely interesting *Encyclopaedia of English Furniture* (Benn), Mr. Oliver Brackett points out that cabinet-making went through a transitional stage in the reign of Henry VIII, when Renaissance details began to be blended with Gothic, and that the former style was fully developed by the time of Elizabeth. He attributes the evolution partly to a change in the outlook of the people during this period from one of war and unrest to one of peace. Internal faction and civil war had caused the nobles to build their homes as fortresses and to have furniture which could be moved easily as each new emergency occurred, whereas now the large country mansion was beginning to be built, and some of the cream of Italian art was having its influence on English architects and designers.

The development was slow but steady, showing itself at first in the stately mansion rather than in the cottage home. Oak remained the staple wood for cottage furniture, but walnut was now greatly favoured for the "more exclusive" pieces in the mansions. Furniture remained heavy, but it was becoming more elaborate in design and workmanship. The detail in much of the ornate inlay work on the panels of the chests and cupboards, and the extravagance of the carving of chair-backs, bedsteads, wall-panelling, and chimney-pieces show that the cabinet-maker must have reached an extremely high standard of craftsmanship such as can seldom have been surpassed, even though later periods may often reveal a more attractive style.

If the Tudors saw the start of the recognised cabinet-maker it was the Restoration, with its invigorating influence, that brought about the revolution in his work. The introduction of foreign ideas by some of Charles II's mistresses, according to Mr. Brackett, played no small part in speeding the change. Perhaps it was jealousy that prompted poor Nell Gwyn to vie with some of her rivals to see who could provide the most luxuriously furnished home. Why, it is recorded that Nell even commissioned foreign craftsmen to execute much of the work in her determination to introduce Continental ideas and not be outdone by a

E

certain French lady who was greatly in favour with the King. Even Catherine of Braganza, the King's lawful wife, brought styles from her native Portugal, while William and Mary, not long after, added to the external influence by favouring Dutch styles.

At no other time, I suppose, has foreign influence played so large a part. The result was a complete uplifting of the minds of the upper classes. Their whole attitude appears to have changed entirely within the space of but a few years. From a spirit of just "making do" they suddenly gained a feeling and desire for comfort. The solid oak chairs felt harder to the seat, and gave way to a more delicate padded chair, often fashioned in walnut or some other wood; it became more comfortable to have a bureau or special writing-table instead of using the heavy "general purposes" dining-table; the chest was no longer found so convenient for *everything*, so the tallboy and chest-of-drawers came into being. Many and varied were the pieces now made, and each assumed a lighter and more elegant style.

The cabinet-maker no longer kept his work within the limits of dire utility. He worked in many woods now, and he introduced glass into some of his pieces, such as in the doors of cabinets and corner-cupboards. He took a pride in experimenting with new ideas and in the blending of different fashions, and he made two great discoveries which were soon to widen the scope of his work—the practice of veneering his furniture and the principle of marquetry, the latter coming to him from Holland. Here let me dispel the idea that veneer is a sign of cheap workmanship or the craftsman's way of hiding defects in his wood. Veneering was started as a means of conserving the more precious woods, and enabled beautiful pieces to be made where sufficient quantities of such valuable timber could not otherwise have been spared. It is a highly skilled branch of the craft, and to this day it takes a really good craftsman to do it well. To watch a cabinet-maker building up attractive designs from fragments of veneer, and then polish it until it has a surface like glass, is an object-lesson in craftsmanship. At any rate, it is a process which the greatest masters have adopted and which has maintained a strong influence from the start.

While the revolution in furnishing was taking place an equally drastic, if slower, change in architecture was being brought about by the genius of Sir Christopher Wren, and by the great wood-carver, Grinling Gibbons. But, though the fashions changed rapidly among the aristocracy, it was some time before they affected the villager. The country cabinet-maker had a difficult part to play, for he had not the facilities for making so great a change with such speed, nor, at first, could he make new styles of furniture at a price the average countryman could afford. Of necessity, therefore, he was often a slow starter where change was concerned. He did not neglect to study these new styles, however, and, in his turn, he did much to influence the outlook of the middle and lower classes in much the same way as the great architects, wood-carvers, and town cabinet-makers had already influenced the aristocracy.

The luxurious models which were being made for the stately homes were often far from suitable for the average, and more humble, country houses and cottages. Yet a change in style was needed in the country too. Thus, the village cabinet-maker had to design pieces suitable to his particular community, yet in harmony with the times. His work may have been less glorious, but it was hardly less skilled, and it certainly displayed a sound understanding of the trend of affairs and of the needs of his locality. Examples of the work of these early country craftsmen reveal a marked individuality.

Many of our leading cabinet-makers and furniture designers, whose influences are felt to this day, were the sons of village craftsmen, and they may even have worked in the country themselves before they achieved fame. William Kent was the son of a Yorkshire coach-painter; the great Chippendale probably learnt the fundamentals of his craft from his father, a joiner on a country estate, before being apprenticed to a London firm; and Sheraton, it is known, was once a country cabinet-maker in the county of Durham.

Few men in any sphere have done more to raise the standard of crafts-manship than Chippendale, Sheraton, and Hepplewhite, as can be seen by the fact that, with their arrival, furniture styles became known after them instead of after the reigning monarch as hitherto. Their names remain famous to this day; their work is still prized in both England and America; and even now their pieces hold sway with many of our present-day craftsmen, some of whom base many of their ideas on their work.

It is to Chippendale that greatest credit might, perhaps, be given, for he was the first of the three, and a number of authorities have expressed the view that his blending of many cultural ideas into one single theme was the work of a genius. Yet there are plenty who prefer the more delicate work of Hepplewhite or Sheraton, who followed him in quick succession. Though much of the earlier furniture was often delightful, it can surely be said with truth that it was in the latter half of the 18th century that the cabinet-maker found his greatest glory. It was not for nothing that this period became known as she "Golden Age of cabinet-making." What more beautiful object can there be than a Hepplewhite chair with its graceful lines, a Chippendale table with its ball and claw feet, or the magnificent inlay work of a Sheraton sideboard? These craftsmen may not have made half the pieces that are generally credited to them, but they certainly made many of them and they were designers on a liberal scale, whose work was, and still is, frequently copied.

An old trade card of Sheraton's reads: "T. Sheraton, 106 Wardour Street, Soho, 1795. Teaches Perspective, Architecture and Ornament. Makes Designs for Cabinet Makers and sells all kinds of drawing books."

Nor were they the only skilled cabinet-makers of this period. The great architect, Robert Adam, also designed much excellent furniture, and there were William Bennett, Ince, Manwaring, Mayhew, Johnson, Shearer, and others.

Unfortunately, however, they appear to have left few behind them to follow their lead. The Golden Age was followed by the Victorian era of ugliness with nothing to commend it in either style or design—an epoch that can hardly be said to have been improved upon by the production of present-day chromium-plated furniture.

Yet, when grace and beauty of design left us with the 18th century, the craftsman did not go with them. In spite of all its ugliness, it can never be said that the Victorian furniture was anything but well made. It was design that was lacking, not workmanship. The same applies to-day. There are cabinet-makers in both town and country who are capable of the highest standards, and many of them are turning out excellent work (58). It is difficult for them to set up a tradition, however, or even to follow an old one, in an age when there appears to be little real stability in either design or architecture. Given the chance, they would prove their worth.

Throughout the centuries the architect and cabinet-maker have gone hand in hand, whether it be for the large London mansion or for the small country cottage. It is the only hope of real success for either, but it is hard to believe that such can be possible again until the days of unrestricted jerry-building are ended and a larger proportion of houses are well designed once more. It is to be hoped that the return of peace will bring with it that greater stability so necessary to both.

CABINET
MAKING:
A Modern Cabinet
Maker at work
constructing a
Gramophone Cab·
inet out of old
wood

59. BLACKSMITH:
A Village Crafts-
man with a piece
of Decorative
Work which he
has made in his
spare time

60. BLACKSMITH:
Old style, working with Hand Bellows

61. BLACKSMITH:
Modern style, Craftsmen seen making a good weld of a broken Lorry Axle

V

THE VILLAGE "MUSKETEERS"

WHILE the potter, weaver, and cabinet-maker fall into a group of their own as being fundamental to the arts, five other craftsmen—the blacksmith, wheelwright, carpenter, saddler, and thatcher—were once the staple workmen of every village. Together with the builder (who by constructing the dwellings for the people brought habitation to the locality in the first place) they could practically guarantee the independence of any rural community in days when men produced all their own food and lived largely by their work on the land.

It is hard to regard the builder as a country craftsman any longer, for he has changed so greatly in the last century or so. Where is there craftsmanship in building houses on mass-production lines out of machine-made bricks? True, plenty of houses are still well designed, but they form a small minority, and they are seldom the work of the country craftsman now. Perhaps I am prejudiced by a love of the Tudor, Queen Anne and Georgian periods, but I can see little beauty or craftsmanship in blocks of uniform structures, of ill-conceived design—if design it can be called—and badly chosen materials, which so frequently desecrate the countryside, and I doubt how many will stand the strain of four centuries as have some of our Tudor cottages.

But the country builder was once a fine workman, and I mention him here for his past glory and for the important part he has played in village life. From the earliest days of civilisation in England, he was the very core of every community. Life and work did not start in any area until he had first put up the homes for the people to live in. He used only local materials for his work, and this, together with his natural sense of the artistic, enabled him to keep the most humble hovel in tone with the district. Even the earliest builders, who felled and cleft oak trees to make a framing for their wattle-and-daub walls, and their descendants, who later discovered that they could construct houses of mud alone, worked with both skill and artistry.

It must have taken a deal of enterprise to puddle chalk and mud with the feet, and then, using only a small hand-fork, to build solid walls of it, scraping them clean and flat with a spade when they were partially dry. The carpenter made the roof framing and the thatcher covered it with straw, and the result was attractive and sound, as can be seen from the cob cottages still standing in Devon and Cornwall to-day. If those builders lacked knowledge of comfort and sanitation, their workmanship was good, and it showed a steady improvement through the centuries down to the Georges.

While the builders made the homes the others did almost everything else that really mattered. The builder was the hub of the community; the others the main spokes, stretching out to serve its many and varied needs.

The Village Blacksmith

Most famous of all was the village blacksmith (27), whose work has been praised in song and verse. The object of legends, superstitions, and customs, he is hailed in many lands as the symbol of English country life. His smithy is by no means always situated under the spreading chestnut tree, nor is he invariably the "mighty man" that the song would have us believe, but the clanging of his hammer on the anvil is a sound that is unique and one that never changes. The inside of his smithy is dirty with grit and grimed with smoke, but in such settings even grit and smoke have a certain charm.

The blacksmith has not earned his fame for nothing. From the start he has shown a mastery of his materials such as can never have been surpassed, while surely no craftsman can have covered so wide a field of work. If he did little more than fashion decorative articles of gold in the Bronze Age, he was already a man of many parts by the Iron Age when he worked with hammer and anvil in much the same way as his modern counterpart. The discovery of metals at this period undoubtedly caused something of a revolution in the mode of living. It meant just the difference between work and toil, for, as we have seen, when all tools had first to be cut from flint before any kind of work could proceed, it must have been toil indeed. In such conditions man was naturally content to labour for his mere existence, and he did not seek, nor want, new channels. Now, however, it was different. Serviceable tools could be made which would do everything with greater speed and less energy. Forests were soon being cleared, and more land was laid down to food production. Settlements were built, and man led a more organised kind of life and developed his barter trade. Competition started. One community would specialise in a certain line, and would exchange part of its produce for that grown by another settlement. An export business developed between communities on much the same lines as that between nations to-day.

And the blacksmith played the principal role. Without his versatility in learning to master his metals, and to forge everything that was required, from a scythe to a nail, this evolution could never have been. Specialist smiths sprang up who worked together in bands, one band making scythes, axes, saws, and other implements; another specialising in weapons and armour; a third band making clocks; and so on. All were essentially smiths, working on the same principles but in different lines, and sometimes in different metals, and they started the many metal trades in existence to-day such as those of the goldsmith, locksmith, gunsmith, clockmaker, and others. It was a clockmaker of 1400 B.C. who is said to have invented the spring which plays so important a part in mechanism now, and through him came the springsmith's trade. He made his discovery when he bent a piece of wire round a rod and noticed its power of resistance. Many of our parish church clocks are the work of early village blacksmiths. The great Tompion was a village blacksmith in Buckinghamshire before he became the finest clockmaker of the 18th century.

Thus it can be seen that the smith became a leading figure in any community as early as the Iron Age, and so he continued until the mechanisation of farming. By the time of the Conqueror his craft was old-established. Smithies had been built in many parts, and in them ploughshares and other implements were forged and oxen were shod for work in the fields. Little more than 200 years later there were sometimes as many as two smithies serving one village, attending to all agricultural needs, shoeing animals on yearly contracts and making articles at ridiculously low prices. A hammer would be forged for a penny, it is recorded, or a billhook for as little as sixpence.

The blacksmith probably knew more about country life by now than anyone else in the district. He understood agriculture almost as well as the farmer, and by his knowledge he was able to design implements to meet special needs; he studied anatomy before ever he shod his first horse or ox, for shoeing can so easily cause injury to an animal; and he tended the needs of wheelwrights, carpenters, and other workers who were so constantly requiring special appliances. The womenfolk, too, appreciated his worth, and made many demands on his service. He was the metal doctor of the village—working mainly for the farm, but also doing numerous other types of work and turning his hand, in his less busy periods, to making such articles as fire-baskets for the home. Although he often introduced remarkable artistry into such work, it was not until the 17th and 18th centuries that he really came forward as an art-metal worker. Then his craft was to undergo a great revolution under the influence of a Huguenot refugee, Jean Tijou, who began forging the glorious wrought-iron work such as is to be found in St. Paul's Cathedral, Hampton Court, and in many churches, country houses, and public buildings throughout the country.

Village blacksmiths were inspired to new possibilities, and many now took up decorative work in earnest (59). A few, like Bakewell, who hailed from Derby, and Edney, who had his forge at Bristol, became masters of the work, and devoted their whole time to turning out superb wrought-iron gates, stairways, and balconies which were eagerly bought up by architects and which became fashionable for both town and country mansions. The blacksmith, with his simple hammer, chisels, and anvil, had set a new style in house design to which no words can really do justice. If only a few were able to reach the standards of Bakewell or Edney—whose works were in a class of their own—a fashion was set, and to this day humble village blacksmiths frequently turn out ironwork which is appreciated by architects of high standing, not only in England but as far afield as America.

A man who can heat solid bars of iron and then hammer them into whatever shapes he likes, and weld, rivet, or bolt them together into models of such artistic perfection, relying almost entirely on his eye for measurements, can surely have no superiors in craftsmanship. It is his very skill in fire-welding together two pieces of iron that distinguishes good from indifferent work, and which is the key to the uniqueness of his craft (60, 61). He must bring his iron to the highest temperature it will stand without burning or disintegrating, and yet be sure that it is hot enough for him to fuse the two pieces into one. A fraction of a second's delay in whipping them out of the fire and hammering them together on the anvil means the failure of a weld.

No other craftsman has to make such instantaneous decisions or take such sudden and violent action upon his materials. A woodworker can put everything down and begin again where he left off, but with a smith it is often a case of now or never. This factor, together with his complete mastery of horses during shoeing, probably accounts for that

62. ABEL PEIRCE AT WORK AT 95:
A typical Old Wheelwright at Arundel, Sussex

63. A WHEEL-
WRIGHT'S YARD

64. WHEEL-
WRIGHTING:
Making a Hub by
Hand

direct downright independence which is so familiar a feature of this craftsman.

Perhaps it is the traditional spirit, too, and the atmosphere of his workshop—not infrequently an atmosphere in which history lingers—that prompts such workmanship and such versatility. Many of our present-day blacksmiths are carrying on a family job that has been handed down from generation to generation for hundreds of years, while their smithies also are often centuries old and must have many an interesting story to tell if only their walls could speak.

Those who revel in anecdotes of the past as I do should never pass a smithy without calling in to see what yarns it has to offer. They may not always convince you, but at least they will entertain you and give you food for thought. There is a little smithy in Yorkshire where, it is said, the axe was forged for the execution of Charles I, and there are others in some of the midland and southern counties where his son, Charles II, is reputed to have taken his horse during his famous flight after the Battle of Worcester. The villages where Queen Elizabeth's horses are popularly supposed to have cast a shoe are almost as numerous as the beds in which she slept, but some smithies are undoubtedly justified in claiming her patronage .There is another interesting old forge at Findon, in Sussex, where, in 1867, Hermit, the only horse ever to win the Derby in a snowstorm, was shod. Nor must we forget the smithies along the Great North Road. Many of them claim to have been visited by Dick Turpin on his ride to York. And what of Gretna Green, the sanctuary of eloping couples?

The smith has many superstitions and customs connected with his trade. They are too numerous for me to tell you, but here is just one piece of tradition with a topical twist, relating to Sussex, Hampshire, and, I believe, Kent. In these districts a few blacksmiths still follow a custom dating back to the Armada—that of firing the anvil to announce the end of war. In those earlier days when we were threatened by invasion a plan was arranged whereby blacksmiths on certain areas where communications were especially bad were to pass on invasion warnings to the outlying villages by igniting gunpowder on their anvils, thus making a report which, in a favourable wind, could be heard 10 miles away. When the invasion never came the blacksmiths decided to rejoice over Drake's victory in this way instead, and so since then the end of every war has been signalled on the anvil. There is a blacksmith at Petworth, now retired, who will tell you how he fired his anvil after the Boer

War, and there are villagers who will vouch that the first indication they received of the end of the 1914–18 war was when they heard the explosion from the nearby smithy.

Perhaps it is a fitting tribute to the craftsman that the horseshoe should so long have been held as the emblem of luck. Yet, if it has brought luck to others it has not left much for the blacksmith. His has been a hard lot this century. All too many smithies have closed their doors since the start of mechanised farming, and the ranks of this fine craftsman have been sorely thinned. It is not that his work has deteriorated or that he is one whit less versatile. He is simply no longer so indispensable.

With the help of the Rural Industries Bureau, however, who have done much to train the blacksmith to meet modern needs, and enabled him to equip his workshop with a few light machine-tools and acetylene welding plant, many are now taking their place in the scheme of things again. The exigencies of war called out for the blacksmith once more, and he was needed to tend agricultural implements as in the past. By his skill and knowledge he answered the call in no small way, and helped the country's farming policy in great measure. Thus he proved that there is still a place for him in even a mechanised world.

Surely the blacksmith must always have an important place in English country life, provided that he studies modern needs and modifies his work accordingly. He is an artist-craftsman of the best type, as capable of fine architectural work as of tending the needs of farmers, and it is to be hoped that full advantage will be taken of his capabilities in both spheres in the post-war reconstruction.

The Wheelwright and Carpenter

Just as the blacksmith was the metal doctor of the community, so, from earliest times, the wheelwright and carpenter have been equally responsible for the woodwork. The wheelwright served the needs of the farmer and of transport (28, 29), and the carpenter looked after home requirements, frequently working in conjunction with the builder.

There were wheelwrights in the Bronze Age who fashioned ploughshares of wood and who made their wheels in the form of solid blocks, and who built carts of osiers covered with hides. There were carpenters, too, working with flint implements even before that. Both craftsmen have been indispensable ever since. The wheelwright it was who built the chariots and thereby started transport at the time of the Romans, the greatest of all road-makers, and but for the carpenters we could never have had woodwork in our homes.

From the time when the wheelwright first conceived the idea of building a cart on the same principles as a sled down to the advent of the motor-car his was a craft of the first importance, in which the utmost skill and enterprise were mingled with a superb mastery of materials and understanding of requirements. Probably no craftsman shows such traces of the old community spirit in his work as he, for he, more than anyone, has always had to work to suit the specific needs of the land in his locality. A cart that would be serviceable in one area might be quite useless on another type of ground, while the peculiar work for which a waggon is required has also to be studied. It is possibly true to say that no two wheelwrights have ever built a waggon *exactly* alike, and to this day almost every county maintains its special design. There is the hermaphrodite in Lincolnshire, the Woodstock in the Chilterns, the tumbril in Norfolk, and so on. These, and many others, were designed by wheelwrights generations ago and, with modifications, have been made traditionally ever since—each still unbeatable for its special needs and locality.

Although serviceable carts have been made since prehistoric times, it was not until the 18th century that the broad-wheel variety that we know to-day came into being, and it is recorded that the innovation caused such an uproar in the country that it became a campaigning point in a parliamentary election, the candidates in one division standing either for or against the change, those in favour of it being pelted and hooted! Nevertheless, the broad wheels won the day, and so the wheelwrights settled down to constructing the waggons which, until recent times, were so familiar but which now, unhappily, are rapidly becoming a thing of the past in many areas, as more and more carts are machine-made in the factory and as new forms of transport are introduced to the farm. Only in a few of the principal farming areas, such as East Anglia and the West Country, are carts still made by wheelwrights. Their yards may still be open in many places but, in most cases, the wheelwright will be found doing repair work or making gates, wheelbarrows, hen-coops, beehives, or ladders. Never pass a yard without looking in, though—just in case there should be a waggon job on hand, for it is hard to imagine anything more interesting, and nowhere is finer craftsmanship to be found.

A wheelwright once told me that 5 years would be extremely quick for a man to learn his work, and that he did not consider that anyone could really master the craft under about 10.

Like most craftsmen who work in timber, the wheelwright buys his ash, elm, and oak in the woods, and has it carted to his yard (63). There he carefully examines each piece and allocates it for the various branches of his craft. The ash he will set aside for the waggon-shafts and for certain parts of the wheels, but the oak he will treasure for the sections getting the greatest strain, such as the wheel-spokes. He measures his wood off carefully, gauging as accurately as possible how much allowance to make for shrinkage during seasoning, and I am told that it takes years of experience before a craftsman can do even this without considerable wastage. No other woodworker pays such special attention to the grain. When the shipwrights built the "wooden walls of England" the lines of the ships depended almost entirely upon the carefully selected branches and boughs of the trees. This same careful selection is just as essential for the strength of the farm-waggon, with its curved body and shafts and, to a lesser extent, for the making of gates and fencing where the oak is cleft or riven rather than sawn.

When the timber has been carefully allocated, it is sawn into various shapes and stacked to season for several years—one year for every inch thickness of wood. In the old days all the timber was laboriously sawn in pits (35)—one man above and the other below—by sawyers. Now it is done by machinery—to the betterment, I gather, of the language and temper of all concerned!

The pride of the wheelwright has always been in his waggons, and it is a remarkable fact that these craftsmen have never used plans or blueprints to guide them in their work, even though much elaborate detail goes into their making. The work is done in truly traditional style. Every piece of woodwork, from a strut to a floor board, has to be carefully planed and then squared or bevelled as required. When the timber is prepared it is mortised or jointed where necessary and bolted together in the square without any attempt yet being made at shaping. The wheelwright builds his waggon in three separate parts—the fore-carriage, hind-carriage, and body—and assembles them when all are complete.

The shafts he shapes by draw-knife, and the wheels he makes dish-shaped to ease the strain on the spokes and to prevent the wheel crumpling up or turning inside out like an umbrella when the hot iron cools

65. WHEEL-
WRIGHTING:
Knocking in the
Spokes

66. WHEEL-
WRIGHTING:
Filing the Spokes

67, 68, 69. WHEELWRIGHTING: Tyring a Wheel

and contracts after tiring. The ends of the front axle he curves downwards slightly so that the front wheels are further away from the body at the top than at the bottom, thus giving a wider lock for turning. And when he dishes these two wheels he must pay special attention to see that he gets just the right angle to ensure that the weight falls vertically upon the spokes at their lowest point.

Most wheelwrights turn their hubs or stocks on a lathe now, but until quite recently they used to chip them out of solid blocks of elm or oak (64). The felloes (pronounced "fellies") too were hewn into their curved shapes by axe and adze, and the spokes were fashioned by drawknife. Some wheelwrights still work in this way, but machine tools are more generally used these days. The spokes are tenoned into the stock (65) and the felloes are drilled on the inside for fastening over the tapered ends of the spokes. When the wheel is finished and trimmed up (62, 66) it is sent to the blacksmith for tiring (67–9). The iron hoop is fired until the heat expands the metal sufficiently to allow the tire to slide comfortably over the wheel, and when it is in place, water is poured over it to make the tire contract again and grip the wheel firmly. It is a fascinating stage to watch—if you can see it through the dense clouds of steam—and to listen to. As the spokes become firmly bedded in under the intense pressure of the contracting iron, a series of sharp cracks and squeaks volley forth until it is hard to imagine that there can be any wheel left!

When each section of the waggon is completed and the whole is assembled the wheelwright sets to work shaping it from stem to stern into the graceful lines so greatly admired by the country lover. No finer example of traditional craftsmanship can be found than this. Every stroke he makes with draw-knife or chisel he carries out with a definite object—to reduce the weight for the horse, to make easier handling for the carter, or to ensure good balance. From start to finish the wheelwright's sole aim is to build a waggon with the minimum of weight, the maximum of strength, and the easiest possible handling capacity. If his lines have grace they have been cut for a reason of usefulness and not for ornament. And that *is* craftsmanship. Even the heaviest farm-cart—painted as only the wheelwright or coach-painter knows how in the traditional colours of the district—has a dignity surpassed only by the old landaus, post-chaises, sulkies, or the very "racy" perch-phaetons of the town coach builders. But many a wheelwright has made these, too, in bygone days.

F

If the wheelwright's work is often the more attractive, the carpenter's is no less useful. Both have always been fine craftsmen, and to this day there is a spirit of friendly rivalry between them, each regarding his craft as the superior. It is unfair to make comparisons. The carpenter's jobs are legion, and often uninteresting to the casual observer, but all call for skill. Work done well by a carpenter will often go unnoticed, but if it was badly done it would be an eyesore. Thus his efforts are inclined to be noticed only when they are bad! Yet, because of his greater variety of work, he has perhaps been of more lasting importance to the community than the wheelwright, for carpenters can still be found working in villages where the wheelwrights have had to close down long ago through lack of business resulting from the changing conditions.

THE SADDLER

No less important has been the saddler, who did all the leather work for the community, except the making of the boots and shoes, which was the province of the cobbler. Like that of the wheelwright, his craft probably did not really develop until the time of the Romans, but there were leather workers, who twisted thongs and passed the ends through deer antlers to form one-piece reins and bridle-bits with the antler serving as the cheek bar, thousands of years before that and long before even the blacksmith first appeared on the scene. Perhaps the craft started in Ancient Egypt, for there were undoubtedly saddlers among the Pharaohs.

It is no exaggeration to say that the saddler has existed in some form in England ever since man first started to move about other than on his own feet (26). There may not have been much refinement about his work then, but by the Middle Ages, when men were starting to take long journeys on horseback, the saddler took an infinite pride in making the trappings. Every village had its quota of such craftsmen, who looked after the needs of farmers and transport alike and who delighted in introducing a localised individuality into their work in much the same way as the wheelwright, so that each district had its peculiar style of trappings and leather-work, as varied as the waggons themselves.

The saddler's work fell into three classes—harness-making, saddlery, and collar-making—and a good craftsman would take as keen a pride in making a heavy farm collar as in sewing the elegant harness for the

o. SADDLERY:
Making Heavy Farm
Saddlery

71. SADDLERY:
Stitching Farm
Harness

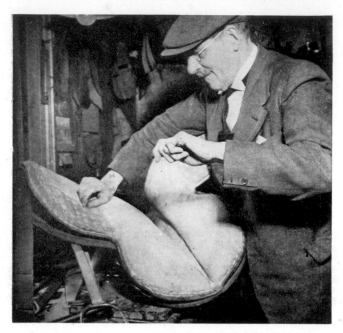

72. SADDLERY:
Lining a Saddle

73. SADDLERY:
Restuffing a Horse
Collar

coach-and-pair, or in making the light saddles for the jumping or trotting classes of the show ring.

It took seven years to make a skilled saddler. For the first 12 months he would learn to make and wax his threads evenly out of his many sizes of hemp, and to stitch neatly. Even sewing is the trade-mark of a good craftsman, and woe betide the saddler who would make "dead men" by sinking his stitches below the surface of the leather! From the start he was taught to keep his needle-holes as equidistant as possible, the length he must make each stitch being marked off for him on his leather by means of a pricking-iron. The number of stitches to be sewn would vary from 6 to 16 to the inch, according to the nature of the work. Later he would learn to cut his leather in such a way as to ensure that when he made up his harness or saddle the most substantial parts of the hide would always form the sections subjected to the hardest wear. Not until he had thoroughly mastered these two essentials would he be allowed to try his hand at making the traces for farm-horses. Then, gripping several thicknesses of leather in his clam, he would sew them together with row upon row of stitches. An untidy row might really have served equally well, but no master saddler worthy of the name would pass anything but a line that was almost a geometrical precision. Such was the pride of the craftsman, and it was a justifiable pride, for leather-work, if it is to be serviceable, must be well made. In a sense, the efficiency of a horse depends largely on a saddler. A well-fitted collar (73) means a good draught, and therefore lighter work for the horse and hours saved for the farmer. But a good collar loses many of its advantages if it has badly made harness to go with it.

It is difficult to tell which is the hardest part of this wide and varied craft. Some will say that only the most skilled can make a comfortable saddle (70, 72), while others will argue that the finest workmanship goes into the harness (71), the cutting of those neat patterns of diamonds being an art in itself. Who will deny that either demands craftsmanship of the highest standard? Yet I am inclined to think that the making of the humble farm-horse collar is as interesting as any of the saddler's work (73).

There is a special collar for every breed of horse, and many a country saddler has more than one breed in his district. Usually he will make his collar in two pieces—the forewale and the body. To make his fore-wale he will sew up a long strip of wide leather into a tube, leaving one edge of the seam extending considerably beyond the other to form the barge. Then he will carefully prepare a quantity of reed about 9 inches long—combing it with a wire brush and damping it—and ram it firmly into his wale by means of a narrow iron bar. When the wale is tightly packed, he will place it on a special block and beat it by mallet into the shape of a collar before stitching together the two ends. For the body he will make a leather throat-piece and stitch it (71), together with one edge of a piece of woollen cloth, to his barge. After splicing together two or three handfuls of reed at the butt ends, he will place them in the throat and lace them over. Then, holding his collar over his knee, he will stuff the body tightly (73), shaping it by eye as he proceeds. When the body is complete he will cut out his leather afterwales, damp them, and sew them to the body with white leather laces.

If his collar is of the closed-top variety, the work is now finished, but buckles and straps must be sewn on to an open-top type, and haines must be fitted. The saddler will do all this—and much more besides, for these are only the elements of collar-making—by eye, making only bare measurements when preparing his materials in the first place.

Unhappily, you will only find saddlers doing this work in very few areas now. It is the usual story—the machine. The fine old craft is dying out, and most saddlers are spending their time on repair work, and making trunks, money-pockets for bus conductors, and numerous trumpery articles where fine workmanship is wasted.

It is not so long though since the saddler's work was the pride of the village. To the end of the last century he was doing delicate work for tandems, pairs, and four-in-hands. Everyone who owned a horse took the keenest interest in its turn-out, and the saddler showed as much enthusiasm in providing the leather-work as if the horse had been his own. Not so long ago, either, the farmer took a far greater pride in his horses than now. If he was less particular about appearances on the farm, his one ambition was that they should be well harnessed to a good waggon when they went to market, and both saddler and wheelwright could be relied upon not to let him down. What more lovely combination was there than a well-groomed horse, with highly polished leather and brasses, drawing a gracefully carved waggon, richly painted in the traditional colours of the district? Here was teamwork. The traditional features of both waggon and trappings revealed their origin at a glance to all and sundry, and the craftsmen worked together to see that the turn-out from their particular village was always the best.

The Thatcher

And now for the thatcher, that little-appreciated craftsman whose work has been hampered by petty prejudices for so long. It may well be that he can justly claim a longer service to the community than either the blacksmith or the wheelwright, antedating even the builder, and invaluable to both home and farm life from the beginning. There is little doubt that thatch of a kind was a principal feature of the earliest form of hut dwelling of which we have knowledge ever made in England. Long before houses had walls, homes were built of grass turves or heather worked into a framework of tree-trunks and twigs, the huts taking the form of bell-tents with the thatch reaching to the ground. Messrs. Batsford and Fry, who, in *The English Cottage*, show so admirably the part the thatched roof has played in the evolution of the cottage, regard this as the most primitive form of roofing, dating back some 10,000 years. Quite possibly it is even older.

Since Anglo-Saxon times thatch has been one of the most popular forms of roofing in country areas, used in olden days for churches and castles hardly less than for cottage homes (15), and maintaining much of its popularity in southern England down to the middle of the last century. In a few areas—notably in East Anglia, the West Country, and in Dorset and Wiltshire—thatching is still greatly in evidence. In other parts it is a dying craft, I fear. The Victorians, who succeeded in banishing beauty from this country in so many ways, hastened its doom by their exaggeration of the fire risk and by their misplaced notion that the thatch was a sign of poverty. And so a great feature of the countryside lost much of its popularity and, in place of the thatched roof—which was always picturesque and which still has the great advantage of rendering a house warm in winter and cool in summer—machine-made tiles—often out of tone with their environment, began to defile the countryside. Victorian clergy ripped the straw from their churches and regarded their actions as progress. In reality, it was the beginning of the decline of a fine and useful old craft, and the number of thatchers has decreased alarmingly ever since, until a thatched roof is now becoming almost a rarity in many areas where once it had been a common sight.

However, the decline is not yet beyond hope, and there is now a possibility that the work will regain much of its lost popularity after the war. The question of making greater use of this kind of roof as a feature of post-war building in rural areas is being explored by planning authorities, and in at least one area a county thatching officer has been appointed to investigate the economic aspect of such a scheme, to train more craftsmen, and to improve conditions in the trade generally. If the revival is found possible it will be a useful one.

Of all crafts, thatching is one of the most individual—possibly even more so than wheelwrighting. Thatchers seldom work other than singly (75–8) or, at the most, in pairs. No two houses are ever thatched exactly alike, while styles and materials vary enormously with the localities. The East Anglian craftsman will make his gable sharp and peaked, while the Wiltshire worker prefers to get his more rounded. The treatment of dormer windows and the many styles of finishing, too, differ according to the individual tastes of the craftsman, who usually tries to leave his trade-mark in some way.

The question of materials causes the chief contrast. Each district uses only locally grown materials—reeds, wheat, rye or oat straw, or heather, as the case may be—so that a roof thatched in one area would still invariably have an appearance quite unlike that in another village even if both were done by the same man. In Devon (76) there is the un-threshed wheat straw, grown in the north of the county and known as wheat-reed; Somerset thatchers rely on rye straw; in Essex rushes are used; while in East Anglia we have the famous Norfolk reed, possibly the best of all; and so on.

As one thatcher, whose family has been at the craft since the days of George II, once put it to me, the thatch helps the country to be in keeping with itself. This was especially so in the days when the builder was still a craftsman. Locally quarried stone, coupled with home-grown reed or straw, ensured artistic houses in tone with the district.

Thatching reeds—most straws are loosely known as "reeds" by thatchers—and the spars (76) for fixing them are seldom made by the craftsman. The spars—hazel boughs twisted in a special way into inverted V's—are made by woodmen in their slacker periods, while the reeds are now frequently prepared by machines in one section of the county and stored ready to be transported by road to the spot where thatching is to take place, as and when required.

The preparation of the straw—variously known as yelming, reed-drawing, or gabbling—consists of removing all unsuitable pieces and arranging the strands level. In some districts the craftsmen do this by passing it through their hands; in other areas it is combed or pulled

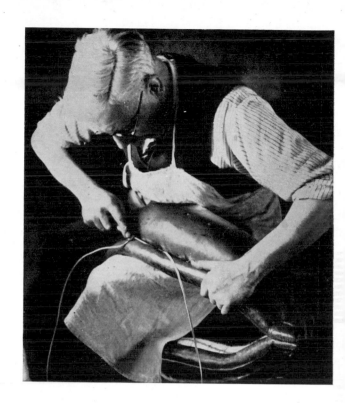

74. SADDLERY:
Stitching a Collar

75. THATCHING:
A Sussex Craftsman
taking his straw up
the Ladder

76. THATCHING:
Beating in a Spar i
Devon

77. THATCHING:
Roofing a Barn with
Home Grown Straw
in Sussex

through a simple kind of press, or even under a hurdle. Although each thatcher has his own style and methods, all work on one general principle. The straw is well damped and is sometimes dipped in alum and size to make it more fire-resisting, and is then carried up the ladder on the thatcher's shoulder by means of a kind of hod.

Thatching starts at the eaves. Bundles of straw are laid pointing upwards and downwards over slats (78), attached horizontally across the rafters, and are raked out to a flat, even surface. In the early days of wattle and daub the thatcher would coat his first layer with a mixture of wet clays and lime to set it. Now, however, he ties it to the slats by twine or wire to make a firm bed on which further bundles can then be laid in tiers—one on top of another—to an incredible thickness, each layer being attached to the one below by means of spars. The spars are placed over and across the bundles and are beaten down hard into the straw by means of a special beater (76).

Each bundle is arranged so that its forward ends are slightly behind those underneath, thus making the thatching line slope upwards and backwards parallel with the incline of the roof, presenting a bristly surface that can be trimmed with shears. Beating plays an important part. The ends of the straw are evened up by hand, and then beaten down with the aid of a grooved beater. Only by continual working with hand and beater can a firm thatch be obtained, and firmness very largely governs the life of the roof. A loose thatch will only let in the rain and make an easier nesting-place for birds. Unless the thatch is made so that the rain will run *off*, rather than *into*, it, rot will soon set in.

After laying on the last of his straw the thatcher "sews" up his roof near the edges, either by plaiting or twisting together strands of straw and pegging them down in lines by spars, or else by criss-crossing two ledgers (pieces of split wood) to form lines of diamonds (dimenting) and fastening them in similar way at the points where they cross. The thatch is now almost as firm as a rock and all that remains is to trim it with shears, lightly brush it, and, perhaps, cover it with a fishing-net as a safeguard against birds and vermin.

The methods of the thatcher are almost as varied as the jobs of the carpenter, and space will not permit giving more than the bare outline of his craft. If he is covering a crofter's cottage he will do the work as simply as possible, often making his thatch in the form of a blanket, sewn together, and held in place simply by weighted ropes slung over the roof. On the other hand, if expense is no object, he will evolve elaborate ways of twisting his straw and finishing off his dormer windows and, instead of simply turning his straw downwards over the point of the roof, he will make a neat "cap" to fit over the top of his thatch to run rom end to end of the house.

There is much that does not meet the eye in thatching, and it is the attention which he pays to the unseen detail that makes all the difference between a good craftsman and a bad one and between a roof that will last and one that will not. A good thatcher will spend as much time fixing the first reeds or bundles as in doing the rest of the roof, for that is his foundation and a thatch with a good foundation may last 40 years or more.

Then we must not forget the hay-rick. Thatch-making machines are tending to oust the hand craftsman from this work now, but until recently the farmer would have been in a sorry way but for the thatcher, who will put almost as much skill into this work as into covering a house roof. To him it does not matter whether it is a house or hay-stack. Either demands good workmanship, and he is out to serve the farmer as much as the home. Such has always been his outlook.

80. HURDLE-
MAKING:
Letting in
a Split Rod

81. HURDLE MAKING:
Weaving the Rods of a Sheep Hurdle

VI

WOODLAND CRAFTS

JUST as a true sailor is lured by the sea, so the woodman could never picture life anywhere but in the woods. Of all craftsmen he sees the beauty of Nature better than any. Its beauty is not lost on him, and I really believe that it often affects his own nature, for a kindlier and happier character I have yet to find.

Two woodmen—father and son—whom I know quite well once told me that it is the quiet, peaceful atmosphere and the independence they like. In such surroundings, they said, work is not work, but a pleasant way of passing the day. There is, indeed, something extremely peaceful about watching the woodman, whether he be hurdler, fencer, or charcoal-burner, or whether he is merely making pergola poles, bean-sticks, or thatching-spars. There is no hustle or bustle. Although he is often working at an incredible speed, you seldom realise it. The song of the birds and the gentle stirring of the trees form a fitting obligato to his work, and everything goes with a swing.

It is difficult to tell which is the oldest of his crafts, but I should say it is a toss-up between hurdle-making and charcoal-burning. Did not the hurdle-maker once play an important part in house construction, and was it not a charcoal-burner, Purkiss, who dragged William Rufus to his hut in the New Forest after he had been shot by the arrow of Sir Walter Tyrrell?

The Glastonbury Lake Village excavations show that there must have been hurdle-makers of a kind as far back as the Early Iron Age, for many of the huts in this settlement were of wattle and daub construction. Wattle hurdles were fixed inside the timber framing of the huts, and were then daubed with a mixture of clay and chopped straw or cow-dung, a method of house construction which was still popular as late as the 16th century. There are a number of interesting examples of this work to be seen in old cottages to this day as Messrs. Batsford and Fry tell in *The English Cottage*.

HURDLES AND WATTLE-FENCING

His work may no longer be used in house construction, but the hurdle-maker yet plays an important part. His is a craft which the machine has not yet found a means of destroying. Largely a southern craft, woven hurdles are greatly favoured by shepherds for penning in their flocks, while wattle-fencing—a more closely woven and superior kind of hurdle to the sheep variety—is used for enclosing estates and private gardens.

Hazel is the most favoured wood, the rich dark variety proving less brittle and easier to work when grown in chalky soil, but the white giving better results in clay districts. Whatever the wood, it must be stacked in the shade during work to prevent sun-baking.

The hurdle-maker must prepare his wood into three different categories—cutting short, trimming, and pointing the thicker branches to serve as the main stakes; merely trimming some of the finer wood; and both trimming and splitting the rest.

Woodmen have individual ways of splitting (79). A tree, felled about 3 or 4 feet from the ground, is used as a splitting-post. The split is started by holding the sharp edge of the fromard against one end of the rod, and tapping the whole down on to the top of the post. Then, carefully working the fromard towards him, using just the correct twist of the right wrist, the woodman gently, but firmly, pushes the rod against the post so that, as the split proceeds, the two sections pass along on either side of it.

It takes about 20 minutes to "weave" a hurdle (80, 81). A curved solid beam, 6 feet long and containing a number of evenly spaced out holes, is fixed to the ground. The hurdler inserts unsplit rods into the two end holes and split ones into each of the rest. Starting 3 or 4 poles from one end, he weaves a few rows of round hazels—known as ethers or round rods—as a foundation, before continuing weaving with his splits. As he lets in each rod he pushes one end downwards into the two preceding rows and, as he approaches the end he twists his hazel right and left—in a way understood only by the woodman—to prevent it cracking on the turn. As each row is finished, he pushes it firmly down with his foot or knee. In a sheep-hurdle he will leave an opening to allow easy handling by the shepherd. The end of the last rod is tucked in; the hurdle is lifted from its frame; and the sharp ends are trimmed off.

82. WEAVING A
SHEEP FEEDING
CAGE

83. THE FINISHED
CAGE is Lifted Out
of the Wheel

84. CHESTNUT
FENCING:
Sawing the Poles

85. CHESTNUT FENCING; Splitting Pales

GATE HURDLES

In some parts, especially in the North and Midlands and in Wales, a gate type of hurdle is made out of willow or ash branches which are lopped in winter and split by means of a frammer or fromard and mallet.

The poles are trimmed, cut to length and mortised. Rails are fitted into the mortises, with an upright pole nailed on as a centre-piece and two braces attached obliquely, one on either side. But this kind is seldom made by the woodman now.

SHEEP FEEDING-CAGES

Although closely akin to hurdle-making, there are now no more than about a couple of dozen craftsmen who can make sheep feeding-cages (82, 83), for so long the favourite of the Southdown shepherd. In the woodland areas of Sussex, Kent, Hampshire and South Wiltshire it is essentially a traditional craft whose secrets have been handed down from father to son for generations.

In spite of the decline, the cages have lost none of their usefulness and through the wartime evacuation of so many flocks from coastal areas to other parts, there are signs that this craft may "rise again." The Southdown shepherd would not be separated from his beloved cages, wherever he might be, and so had them sent to his new abode. Thus, others had the chance of seeing them for the first time, and tried them out with their flocks.

The craft is similar to hurdle-making except that it is carried out on a circle, known as a wheel, which is fastened into the ground. There are 12 holes in the wheel into which the pointed ends of the stakes are driven. Two ethers are plaited together through the stakes at their bases, each going alternately in front of and behind the stakes. After two or three circles, a few rows of "splits" are threaded singly through the stakes to about a third of their height. The top row is nailed to the stakes to prevent slipping, and a space is left in the sides through which the sheep can put their heads to help themselves to the hay.

An iron ring is pushed down taut over the stakes, and the work of plaiting and threading starts afresh above it. Finally, the ends of the rods are cut off to prevent possible injury to the sheep; the top rods are beaten down with a special short crowbar and nailed; the iron ring is released by a patent clip and removed; and the finished cage is lifted out of its wheel (83). The average life of one of these cages is given as about 9 years.

CHESTNUT FENCING

Another interesting craft of the woodman is the making of cleft chestnut fencing—one of the oldest, smallest, and least-known of rural industries(37).

Only in four counties—Sussex, Surrey, Kent, and Hampshire—do chestnuts grow in sufficient profusion for the work. Yet no other tree has the necessary durability, and somewhere about £30,000 is spent annually on the purchase of suitable woodlands for the industry. A plantation is useless for 8 years after felling and so new acres must be worked each year.

Chestnut pales, laced together with wire top and bottom, and sometimes in the centre as well, may not look attractive, but it forms a fencing that will last a lifetime. For that reason, it is exported all over the world.

Nor is it as simple to make as it looks. Two years is a normal time for a woodman to master even the elements of the craft, and each pale represents work stretching over a year. Every stage, with the exception of the final wiring together of the poles and pales, is carried out entirely by hand.

In the autumn the chestnut underwood is cleared about a foot from the ground—only the trained eye being able to detect the best pieces for the job—and the poles are trimmed in the woodland "workshop." These workshops are quaint, indeed. On a framework of newly felled poles the woodman puts up canvas awnings to shield himself from the rain, making a wall of thin branches and twigs on one side as protection against the prevailing wind (86). For hours he will stand in his hut— wet or fine—trimming, splitting, and cleaving hundreds of pales a day. Balancing each pole on a special block, he first removes all small offshoots with his handbill before laying it on a marked table to give him the length to which he must saw it (84). Then he shaves off the bark and smooths and trims the poles again preparatory to stacking. This takes him the five months from November to March, when the poles will be sufficiently seasoned to cleave into pales.

The most skilled part of the craft, and one entrusted to only the most experienced woodman, it is the cleaving which makes all the difference between good and bad fencing (85). The woodman must cleave only stout, straight-limbed poles which, provided that the grain will allow it, will yield pales of not less than 2 inches on the face and $1\frac{1}{2}$ inches on each arris. As with the hurdle-maker, so he must work his fromard with infinite care, keeping his line as straight as possible and avoiding all knots. A really skilled craftsman will cleave as many as 25 pales from each pole, but comparatively few reach that level.

The pales are now pointed (86) and sorted, and dropped into a woodman's "notch" for wiring into bundles by means of a grip, a "notch"-full representing an average length of fencing (87, 88).

The pales are sent away for wiring-up into fences and this is done on one of the most antiquated kinds of machine I have ever seen. The pales are threaded through 2 or 3 pairs of wires—one at each end and sometimes a third in the middle—which are drawn from spools to a drum many yards away. The machine is operated by hand by a man at a bench at one end. Three turns of a handle to the right and the pale is firm. As each is fixed it shoots—perhaps it would be better to say jerks—backwards a few inches, leaving space for the next to take its place.

Whether all wiring is done in this way I do not know, but the one I saw was in the middle of woods, and must really be seen to be believed.

CLOGGING

It is generally believed that clogs are based on the old wooden shoe worn extensively by Dutch peasants, and that they were introduced into this country through the Fens, but it is not known when they were first made in England.

That clogging is an old woodland craft, however, there is no doubt, for it is known that this kind of footwear was fully in fashion by the 13th and 14th centuries when, in spite of their weight, they were greatly favoured by rich and poor alike in country districts. In the 15th century they began to lose some of their popularity with the richer classes who then wore them only in bad weather, and throughout the intervening centuries the clog became more and more regarded as a stamp of poverty until to-day many workers who had once sworn by them have turned to cheap-quality, and far less serviceable, boots.

Yet, although it has declined in popularity, there is still a certain demand for the clog, and the true handcraftsman, with less to do now, is turning out better work to-day than ever.

Lancashire weavers, certain kinds of miners, and the dairy workers of Yorkshire and Westmorland will always, I think, remain faithful to the clog, while there are many who will still firmly declare that the wooden shoe holds a unique healing quality. Whether or not this is merely an old superstition it is hard to say, but old people will turn to a pair of clogs as a cure for weary feet before trying any other remedy, and they will declare quite sincerely that the wood holds some medicinal property. But I have never met anyone who could tell me what that property is or who could produce any convincing proof!

The craft is confined almost entirely to the North and to Wales, and although it has been carried out in other parts in the past—and may still be plied in isolated Midland areas—few people in the South will ever have seen such a craftsman at work.

Most clogs are made of alder or birch, the softness of these woods making the finished article less liable to split when the wearer steps on a stone or other sharp object. As alders are not to be found in any quantity in the North, much of the timber is imported from Wales or Shropshire, where the first stages of the craft are often carried out on improvised benches in the woods. The trees are felled in spring or summer by woodmen living on the spot or by journeymen from the North, and are sawn and split into fixed lengths of four different sizes suitable for men, women, boys, or children.

By means of the clogger's knife—a queer implement, anything up to 3 feet long with a short blade about 4 inches wide set at an angle to the handle and containing a hook at one end—the blocks are roughly shaped into one-piece soles and heels, and are stacked to dry in the open for some months before being sent to the little country workshops to be made up.

The cutting of a clog sole is fascinating to watch. Fastening the hook of his knife to the bench to act as a pivot, and holding his block on the bench with his left hand, the clogger works his knife with his right hand, in much the same way as a guillotine, and moves his block slightly as he makes each fresh cut. He must get just the right bodyweight behind his pressure, and this pressure, together with the angle of his blade, enables him to cut good clean curves of the correct shape. Although it takes considerable practice to know what pressure to exert, a skilled craftsman will work with great speed and will gauge his curves and the

86. CHESTNUT
FENCING:
Pointing his Pales in
his quaint hut

87. CHESTNUT
FENCING:
Placing the
Pales in the
Woodman's
Notch

88. CHESTNUT
FENCING:
Tying th
Bundles i
the Notch b
means of
Grip

89. CHARCOAL BURNING: Old style method in Sussex

amount of wood to cut with almost uncanny accuracy without so much as making a single measurement or mark.

By means of various, shaped knives, he next cuts a grooving round the top edge of the sole, hollows out the instep, and generally shapes the block to the foot. A clog is a succession of curves, and one bad curve can mean acute discomfort to the ultimate wearer.

The leather "uppers" are usually made by a leather worker, such as a saddler or cobbler—although some craftsmen do this work themselves—the most usual type being made in two pieces, which are shaped on a stretching machine and sewn together. The upper is fastened into the groove of the clog sole and a strip of leather is overlaid to make it weatherproof.

Just as the blacksmith must shoe the horse, so must the clog-wearer be shod. Special semicircular irons for the heels and carefully shaped rims for the soles are made by local blacksmiths, and these must be fixed with infinite care to the base by the clogger, who has had numerous styles made for him, and takes infinite care in choosing and fastening the most suitable ones—watching the walk of his prospective customer with just as much attention as the blacksmith will pay to a horse. The irons give balance and poise to the wearer and the craftsman knows that irons that suit one person will not necessarily suit another.

CHARCOAL-BURNING

When Purkiss dragged William Rufus to his hut in the New Forest in A.D. 1100, charcoal-burning had long been a well-established rural industry. Charcoal was the fuel used for the smelting of metals for centuries before coal was ever thought of, the Bronze and Iron Age workers having used it for their metals—a fact borne out by the discovery of charcoal deposits from the fires of primitive man. Wall-writing, too, carried out in this material 2,000 years or more ago gives further proof of age.

The first cannon ever made in England is said to have been made at Buxted, in Sussex, from metal smelted by charcoal heat. In the 16th century, when the industry reached its peak, this woodman was of considerable importance, for without him the great iron foundries of Sussex and Kent, then the main smelting districts, could not have worked. The blacksmith needed charcoal for his forge; the armourer and chain-maker used it; it was burnt in household fires; almost every thing that required intense heat depended on charcoal.

By comparison with other woodmen, the charcoal-burner was prosperous, but he was also a frequent source of anxiety and, according to records of the 16th and 17th centuries, it would seem that we might well have lost Armada and had no woodlands left to us to-day if he had not been taken in hand in time! He could sell his material as fast as he could make it and so he had little respect for laws. Trees were felled in such numbers to meet his needs that there was soon an outcry. Personal letters, written first to Henry VIII and later to Queen Elizabeth, stressing the need to restrict this felling, resulted in a number of Acts being passed controlling the amount of timber to be cut for charcoal-burning in all districts except the great iron-smelting areas of Sussex, Kent, and part of Surrey.

But the woodman almost entirely disregarded these laws until, with the threat of a Spanish invasion ever growing, further agitation was made on the ground that, not only were the forests being seriously bared, but that the timber was urgently needed for ship-building. When later iron smelting moved almost wholesale to the Birmingham area, Warwickshire woodlands suffered a similar fate.

But let us not be too hard on the charcoal-burner. He was constantly badgered by the smelters to produce more and more material and, if he did "go off the rails" a bit, his work has always been good, and it has formed an important and picturesque feature of the countryside.

Most charcoal-burning is done in portable kilns in the woods these days, but there are still a number of woodmen who do the work in the old way (34). Have you ever tried to track one of them down and watch him through the whole process? Once having found him, it may take days to see it all through, but if you *can* spare the time, you will find it most fascinating—especially if you are a bonfire lover like myself.

The principle of making charcoal is to remove all vaporising substances from the wood by burning it at an even temperature and without air. The woodman, who builds himself quaint huts in the woods during burning-time, fells his timber and cuts his "billets" to suitable lengths, usually about 3 feet. With a central stake as the foundation of his "hearth" he builds up his pile by standing his billets on end with a slight lean towards the centre to form a dome about 5 feet high, containing several tons of wood with air spaces evenly distributed throughout (89). The thicker branches are placed nearest the centre with the thinnest on the outside.

The "dome" is covered with grass or straw and then coated with

90. WALKING STICKS: Straightening by "Horse." The Sandbed is seen behind

91. WALKING STICKS: Steaming the Sticks before Curving the Handles

92. HEATH BROOM MAKING IN SUSSEX

93. HOOP-SHAVING:
Henry James Puttick, an 80-year-old craftsman of Sussex

damp earth. The stake is now lifted out and faggots and burning embers are place in the hole to light the fire. The hole, or chimney as it is called, is covered with turf, and burning begins.

The charcoal-burner will watch his fire with as much care as a shepherd will give to his lambs, for the wood must burn evenly throughout to make good charcoal, and never must there be a flame. He must *char* and not *burn* his wood. If there is the slightest breeze he will build windscreens of poles and bracken as a protection, and every two hours, night and day, he will "take a walk round," throwing on a turf here, splashing on water there, and generally tending "soft spots" in his dome. He will generally tell by the colour and volume of the smoke when charring is complete, but if he has any doubt, he will pull out a bottom piece of wood as a test. Then he will throw water on to the pile to drive the steam inwards and put out the fire.

Although the use of coal for smelting has deprived the charcoal-burner of his main importance, there is yet a need for his work.

Charcoal is used in chemicals, in the manufacture of aeroplanes and gas-masks, in explosives, in biscuits, and many other articles. I have even heard of it being used for generating electricity.

If he nearly lost us the Armada, the charcoal-burner has played his part in two great wars. More elusive these days, he takes a bit of finding now, but he can still be seen in the Wyre Forest, in Warwickshire woodlands, in Shropshire, the New Forest, and in parts of the Home Counties. There are direct descendants of Purkiss in the New Forest to-day, but although the family have been charcoal-burners for centuries, and were still engaged at the craft until a few years ago, I am not sure that there are any carrying on the tradition at present.

WALKING-STICKS

Ever since the Flood, it is said, men have carried walking-sticks, and they have been made in the woods for many centuries. The stave gave place to the cudgel, and from these two have gradually developed the many kinds of walking stick we know to-day, ranging from the more "aristocratic" gold-rimmed malacca, made of imported wood, to the heavy country type of ash or thorn or the Scottish crummock.

If the walking-stick has largely given place to the umbrella in towns it is still popular with country folk, and hand-made sticks are exported

H

from the English countryside as far afield as America, New Zealand, Australia, and Africa.

A deal of craftsmanship goes into their making, the work being done partly in the woods and partly in small country workshops, chiefly round the wooded areas of Chiddingfold and Godalming in Surrey, in the Cotswolds, and in parts of East Anglia. Many of the sticks are drawn straight from the woods, but ash plants are also specially cultivated. The cultivation in itself takes considerable skill and knowledge. The ground must be well prepared, trenched, and manured and, in many cases, the saplings are planted in such a way as to force their roots to grow at right-angles to the stem to form the handles, for the connoisseur will maintain that no handle is successful unless it is grown below ground.

It is not really done to ask a craftsman how he brings about this freak growth. He will usually try to keep it a close secret, and will simply smile, remark that it is quite simple, and then change the subject! Roughly, it is done like this. The sapling is uprooted after about two years, and cut short to prevent further growth. A number of small buds will then be found growing out of the stem, and all but the one nearest the stem are nipped off and the sapling is replanted flat in a trench with the bud facing upwards. After three years the bud will have grown into a long stem to form the stick, while the original stem of the sapling serves as the handle. It is not quite as easy as it sounds. Care has to be taken that no other shoots break out and the plantation must be well tended throughout the period of growth. A May frost can easily ruin a whole plantation, so that, if there is any doubt about the weather at that time of year you will find workers lighting smudge fires as a precaution.

When the plants are uprooted the sticks are placed in beds of sand which are heated by ovens below them, the action of the sand rendering them pliable and easily workable. When the sticks are well "cooked" the craftsman takes them, one by one, from the sand and pulls them through a "horse" (90)—a wooden plank with niches cut out of the sides—to straighten them, and it is interesting to see how plastic they have become under the action of the sand. Where crook handles are to be made, one end is immersed in a copper containing hot water, kept to a constant heat by a fire below it, and left to soak for some time (91). This end is then bent round in an iron ring, tied in position, and left standing in another bed of sand to dry and harden. A primitive way of doing this is to place damp moss over the handle end and to suspend the stick between ceiling-beams with a weight attached to the other end.

Frequently sticks are made in two pieces. The handle is then often made of holly, and is invisibly glued and jointed to the stem. When the stick is set the ends and nodules are trimmed off and, in the case of the smarter town types, the whole is scoured and treated with preservative. The smarter the type the more delicate the work.

BESOM BROOMS

Of all brushes, the besom, or birch broom, is probably the oldest form still in use, yet it remains one of the most popular on estates and in private gardens. Although the adjacent villages of Baughurst and Tadley, on the Hampshire–Berkshire border, form one of the best-known centres, besom-making is carried on in many parts of England, both in wooded areas where there is an abundance of birch trees and on sandy commons where heather grows in profusion.

Whether it be birch or heather, the principles of the craft remain the same, although each area has its individual variations of style. While the heather besoms are usually made in cottage gardens near the commons, birch brooms are often made in the woods. The work is highly skilled, and I am told that it takes anything up to 5 years before a woodman can make a good broom (92).

The broom-squire, as this type of woodman is called, cuts his birch underwood in very early spring, just as the sap rises in the stem and just before the buds burst. Here, indeed, he must work with Nature, otherwise his finished broom will either be brittle and "splinter" at the first sweep, or else will lack that pliancy that forms so great a feature of a good broom. After cutting, he stacks his birch in a section of the woods where it will be sheltered from the rain, and yet be well blown by the wind and baked by the sun. Here it must be left to weather for weeks while the bands for binding the brooms are prepared and the handles and fastening-pegs are cut. Withies or ash are used for binding, and these are cut in full foliage, trimmed, split, and placed in a pot of boiling water—often an old gipsy cauldron—for 10 minutes or so to render them more durable by making them first soft and then hard. Although not all makers boil them, many woodmen declare that it makes the easiest and best binding.

Almost any type of wood that will yield stout but not too heavy poles, approximately 3 feet long, is selected for the handles. If a pole is not straight it is either heated and bent so over a turf fire, or else it is trimmed in such a way as to give the finished broom a similar balance and the appearance of being straight. The poles are pointed at one end and shaved smooth, a hole being bored through them near the pointed end for fixing the head.

When the seasoning is finished, the woodman sits on a stool in his hut and arranges his birch twigs into a neat bundle with the longest pieces in the middle. Then, letting his withy band into the centre of the twigs, and gripping his bundle in a vice, he binds it several times tightly round one end of the bundle and pushes the rest of his withy under the bands by means of a stag's antler. He binds his twigs in two places, leaving a space in between, and pushes the pointed end of the handle into the bundle, driving it securely home by knocking the whole on to the top of a chopping-block. The hole in the handle will now be just below the first band, so that an ash-peg or spick can be driven through both the handle and the head to hold them firmly together. A skilled squire will study his user with infinite care, making his handles just the right length, and varying the thickness of his heads to suit the height of the customer.

HOOP-MAKING

You may have to walk through miles of woods these days before you track him down, for the aluminium bucket and other types of metal ware have deprived the hoop-maker of the greater part of his business, even though his hoops are still needed for such articles as beer and fish barrels, for garden sieves, and for wooden tubs.

The old woodman, skilfully cleaving his poles into the greatest possible number of strips and then shaving them on his upright "break" (93) is a rare sight now, but it is one not to be missed. His many ways of bending his rods into circles before fastening them are interesting in themselves, for each needs a sound knowledge of the woods and considerable experience. In Kent or Sussex you will find him curving his rods between two horizontal poles, while in the Lake District you will see how he coils them in a cylinder. In one or two areas he will use an eight-pronged easel. Each prong contains a number of holes into which pegs are put according to the size hoop to be made, and the rod is coiled in the circle formed by the pegs. In some woods you will find the woodman heating his rods over a trestle fire.

Whatever method you happen upon, the hoop-maker will invariably declare that his is the best and quickest. If you want to judge his speed for yourself, a good craftsman should make anything between 400 and 500 hoops in a day.

THE CHILTERN CHAIR-BODGERS

In parts of the thick beech woodlands of the Chilterns are to be found a unique, but rapidly dwindling, band of craftsmen—the chair-bodgers. I do not believe that such craftsmen exist in any other woods in England, yet their work can be traced back (22, 24)—though not necessarily in the Chilterns—at least to the bowl-turners of the Glastonbury Lake Village.

Using the old-fashioned pole-lathe (22), the bodgers work in quaint little home-made workshops dotted about the woods, turning legs and stretches or spars for a Buckinghamshire chair factory. The turned parts of the old Windsor and Wheelback chairs were made in this way, and the bodgers are carrying on the work in traditional style. That their craftsmanship has not deteriorated can be gathered from the fact that legs turned in the Chilterns in recent years have been mistaken for genuine antiques and sold as such, even though the craftsmen themselves have made no attempt at slavish reproduction.

The chair-bodger uses small beech trees, felled by the estate wood-men. He saws the trees into logs of the same length as the parts to be made, and splits them, while still green, by hatchet before trimming them to rough shapes by means of short-handled axes, made specially for the job. Sitting at his shaving-horse, he "rounds" his shapes by draw-knife before turning them on his pole-lathe. Usually he will take about two dozen legs right through all the processes at a time.

Each type of chair needs a different leg, and the bodger works accordingly. A true craftsman, he works on traditional lines, yet refusing to make servile reproductions. Thus he has a style of his own. The craft is old and the craftsmen mostly elderly; many of their patterns date back 200 or 300 years; and the whole setting is old-fashioned. Is it surprising then that their work too often assumes an appearance of age? They are certainly a unique band, capable, I believe, of turning almost anything out of their trees.

But there are not many of them left working in the old style. The younger men prefer to take the wood to workshops and to use power-driven lathes.

By the way, never call this craftsman simply a bodger. He does not like it. The word "bodge" by itself means to make-do, and a bodged piece of work is a scamped affair without real workmanship. So "chair-bodger" in future, please!

Sundry Woodland Jobs

The woodman's work is manifold. Not all his jobs can be dubbed as crafts, yet all require a measure of skill closely akin to craftsmanship and a sound knowledge of materials. All have a fascination of their own.

There is the making of tent- and clothes-pegs, and the cutting and twisting of thatching-spars. Numerous kinds of fire-lighters, such as the bavin, are made by him and, though he may not do this in the woods, it is the woodman who lays the hedges. What more skilled job can there be than this? There is even a knack in twisting the strands of underwood to bind the faggots. If you doubt it, try for yourself, and see how many you split or break!

VII

CRAFTS ESSENTIAL TO OTHER WORKERS

IF the machine developed industry, it was the craftsman who started trade. Just as the blacksmith, carpenter, thatcher, and others formed an interdependent unit so necessary to the village, so craftsmen of various kinds once comprised a closely knit band essential to trade, to farmer, and to other workers.

The weavers and spinners, as we have seen, took their work beyond the confines of their own localities, and built up an export business. But they could not have done this without the carpenter to make the loom in the first place or without the wheelwright to fashion the spinning-wheels. The wheelwright, too, needed the metal worker to make the spindles for his wheels, while he, in turn, relied on the smelter who, likewise, was dependent on the charcoal-burner. So it went on. The saddler would have been idle but for the tanner, and the fruit-grower required baskets to gather his produce for market. The miller called for the millwright. *Everything,* down to a nail, had to be made by hand, so that one craftsman was often dependent on many others before he could even begin his own tasks, and no enterprise of any kind, whether it was for trade or agriculture, could be carried out without the hand worker playing his part somewhere.

With the coming of industrialism, many laborious, but essential, manual jobs disappeared—to the benefit of all. But, though industrialism made work less irksome, it had a disastrous effect in other ways. That old interdependence between craftsman and wage-earner was now carried on as between machines, and many whose skill had enabled them to serve the needs of other callings for so long lost much of their importance. One by one their crafts dwindled or died.

The cooper—once essential to the dairy-worker and brewer alike— found that the tubs which he had made from wood, cleft by himself, could now be turned out by machinery, and the hand-tanner, upon whom the saddler had relied, was replaced in large measure by the factory, where hides began to be treated by modern chemicals instead of by oak bark. Ladder-making, too—necessary to so many types of land work—gradually became more and more the province of the

67

machine shop where the work was done on mass-production lines from imported timber. These, as well as many others, all form skilled crafts—as opposed to the tedious labour of the nail-maker—and their decline is a tragedy.

Yet, in spite of their decline, they are still carried on in various parts, surviving either because the superiority of hand-work is still appreciated by those dependent on the articles or material for their own jobs, or because such articles cannot yet be made by machinery. If the work of these craftsmen is only of strict utility value—and therefore not decorative in the strict sense of the word—it is no less skilled or interest-ing, for an ancient tradition still lingers to keep their workmanship at a high standard.

THE TANNER

Ever since man first killed animals and wrapped himself in the skins to keep warm and to hide his nakedness, there have been tanners who cured the hides to prevent them going bad. Tanning was already a thriving industry by the time of the Conquest, and many tanneries are mentioned in the Domesday Book. As early as the 11th century the hides of oxen, cows, horses, and sheep were used to make leather after being either tanned or tawed, and hides were exported in quite large numbers to other countries.

Exactly how the early tanner worked is hard to say. Quite possibly many of the stages of the industry were very similar, if not identical, to those still practised in some of the few remaining old-style tanneries to-day, for in such places some of the methods appear quite primitive, and are carried out with natural materials of the countryside—lime from the rocks and bark from the trees—in a way that can hardly have been practised less by the prehistoric craftsman who, of necessity, was far more dependent on natural elements.

For centuries every self-supporting village, and certainly every market-town, could boast its tannery (17). Many were run on the feudal system, and there is no doubt that the overlords had a prosperous business, for home-tanned hides held a high value.

A number of factors caused the decline—the coming of industrialism, resulting in the decline of the horse for agriculture and for road travel; the introduction of the factory system; the development of tanneries in other countries reducing our exports; and the advance of science,

TANNING:
Removing the Hides
from the Lime Baths

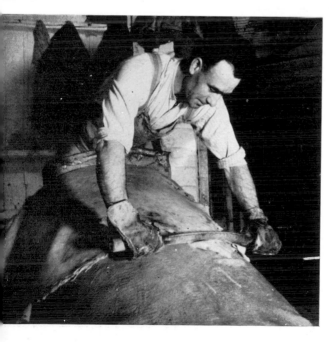

95. TANNING:
Removing the Fatty
Tissues from a Hide

96   TANNING:
Removing the Hi
daily to a stron
Tan Bath. The n
use the poles to p
vent slipping

97.   TANNING:
Removing   Hides
from the Revolving
Drum

causing the substitution of modern chemicals for old methods in order to speed turnover.

There are many old tanyards to be seen still but, alas, few are working. Instead, they lie derelict and decaying—memorials to a once thriving and highly skilled country industry. The work remains just as important, but it is mostly done in the towns now, and by means of machinery and high-speed chemicals. For all that, the work of the hand craftsman is still the best. His leather is more durable and it is greatly favoured by those who will later have to work it, like the saddler, hand-shoe maker, or other high-class leather worker. Skill in tanning will show itself in the finished article and it takes 5 years or more to make a really good craftsman.

Dotted about the country, especially in the old market towns, there are even now a few old-style tanneries still working. You may have to travel miles to find one, but a visit is well worth while. There is an interesting old one at Chichester and another at Redhill. There are smaller ones at Crediton and Colyton, in Devon, and one or two in Lincolnshire, Gloucestershire, and East Anglia.

Roughly, tanning can be divided into two categories—heavy leather workers and light—some firms dealing in the stiffer ox-hides for boot-soles and heavy saddlery; others handling the lighter sheepskins for more delicate work.

Tanning-bark is stripped from the oak trees when the sap rises in April or May, and is placed in an old-fashioned grinding-machine, where slow revolving wheels crush it into small pieces. The tan is extracted by soaking the bark for days in pits of cold water and the liquid is pumped from the pits into the tan-baths as required.

It takes anything up to a year to tan a hide. After rough cleaning, the leathers are placed in lime baths for about a fortnight to loosen the hair and plump up the fibres of the pelt, thus enabling the tan, at a later stage, to fill the fibres to capacity. As each is finished it is "drawn," from the bath by two men carrying poles with special hooks on the end (94), the weight and slippery surface making it impossible to remove them in any other way. Suspending one end of the hide on their hooks they walk the length of the baths pulling it along between them. The drawn skins are placed in a pile ready to be "unhaired" on a scraping machine. Sheepskins, where the wool is valuable, are given a less drastic kind of liming, and the wool is plucked out by hand.

Next comes one of the most difficult parts of the craft—fleshing by

I

hand. Placing his hide over a kind of sloping horse and using a long curved blade, the craftsman stands behind the horse and, leaning downwards over it, cuts away the flesh by long strokes (95). One false stroke means a serious loss in the finished product. Now the hide is scudded in similar way to remove the surface fats from the grain. Some skins are "split" where fineness is required for more delicate work or for the making of parchment or chamois leather. This is done by means of a sharp knife, and it is remarkable the skill which some craftsmen display. The slightest slip and the hide is ruined, yet I once met a tanner who, I was told, had handled as many as 1,200 skins in a week, and could split so finely that it was possible to fold his hide 10 times and read a newspaper through it.

The skins are now "rounded.' Although this stage, comprising cutting away the edges with a sharp knife, appears quite simple, it is highly skilled, for the amount to be cut must be judged accurately. After a thorough washing, when all traces of the lime must be removed, the actual tanning starts. The hides are placed into a succession of baths (96). One edge of the leather is fastened to a stout wooden slat, both ends of which overlap the sides of the bath. In this way numerous skins can be suspended full-length at the same time, and each day the leather is moved up into a bath containing a stronger solution to facilitate penetration of the tan liquor. After many weeks in the baths the hides are placed in an enormous wooden drum and are revolved in a mild dressing solution as a safeguard against oxidisation (97).

The skins are now cured and tanned and are hung up to dry in airy rooms before being oiled by hand (98)—a process which has never varied throughout the centuries—and rolled. Until quite recently this was done by hand too, but machine rollers have now been substituted in even really small tanneries because of the extra weight which it is possible to obtain, some being capable of a pressure of 10 tons.

THE COBBLER

Once a familiar country character, the village cobbler is another who is fast dying out, and his work is but a shadow of its former self. No longer does he make boots and shoes for all and sundry. That work was wrested from him long ago by the factories, while the retail shoe shop has also relieved him of much of his repair work. The old nursery ditty, "Cobbler, cobbler, mend my shoe, get it done by half-past two," has

98. TANNING:
Oiling the Hides.
Women are now
being employed for
this

99. A COBBLER:
Handstitching
Agricultural Boots

100. BASKET-MAKING
A Member of the
Women's Institute
making Potato
Hampers

101. A BASKET-MAKER AT WORK WEAVING A HOUSEHOLD
BASKET
Beside him is a stack of Agricultural Baskets

lost much of its point now that so few children have ever seen a cobbler. Even so, he is still to be found in agricultural villages and small towns, for the farm-worker is as appreciative as ever of his worth and refuses to allow anyone but the cobbler to repair his boots, even if he can no longer have them made by him in the first place as in olden days.

He was once an important link in the village community. The labourer tended the cattle; the tanner cured the hides for the cobbler; and the cobbler, in turn, made them into boots for the labourer, so that often the labourer was wearing the skins of his own animals. Each studied the other's needs and the results were good. The cobbler under- stood agricultural conditions and made his boots accordingly. He would use only the best leather, and his craftsmanship in cutting out the soles and uppers and sewing them together (99), in a way to render such cumbersome articles both comfortable and watertight, was high indeed. The boots were the pride of the labourer, who would set aside part of his harvest money to have a new pair made—looking forward to this almost as if it was an annual treat.

Everyone was dependent on the cobbler, so he often adopted an attitude of good-natured independence himself. He took on an immense amount of work, made no promises when it would be done, yet usually got through his orders with remarkable speed. That attitude of inde- pendence is still to be found in a notice outside a cobbler's shop in Arundel: "Old Harry works here. Repairs Boots and Shoes and is not dear. His leather is good, his work is quick. His profits small, but he gives no tick"—an excellent description of the village cobbler.

WILLOW-GROWING

Since earliest times the basket-maker has served the needs of other workers, but he is dependent on the osier-grower whose work goes back to early Bible days. Delilah bound Samson, we are told, with "seven green withs that were never dried" when she tried to rid him of his abnormal strength; the five thousand were fed from baskets woven from osiers; while the Ancient Britons made shields of withies with which to defend themselves.

Seventy-five per cent of the willows required for basket-making are especially cultivated round the low-lying districts of Langport, Kings- bury, and Athelney, scene of King Alfred's great cooking mishap. Looking down over these wide expanses is Glastonbury, and it is possible that the inhabitants of the Lake Village grew willows here for their basket-making.

Willow-growing is no easy business, good land and considerable skill being needed. The land must not be waterlogged nor contain chalk. A cool, medium-weight, clay soil is ideal. After cleaning and ploughing, the plants, or sets—obtained by cutting off the best lengths from the current year's crop—are carefully pushed into the ground between December and March by experts, an average of about 20,000 sets being needed to plant an acre. In spite of the greatest care being taken in hoeing and spraying during the first year, it is seldom that a crop can be used before the second season. Then the withies are cut by a special hook between December and April—provided serious flooding does not hamper operations too greatly. Only the most experienced workers do the cutting, for even small mistakes can cause considerable damage to a plantation.

After cutting and bundling, the withies are taken to a central point on the water to be transported by boat to the high road, where lorries wait to cart them to the grower's yard. Here they are sorted into lengths ranging from 2 to 8 feet, and graded, when all rough and unsuitable rods are thrown out. The rods are now boiled in a large tank for six hours, after which they are taken to the homes of the women workers to be peeled. After peeling they are a light brown colour, known as buff, and can be worked by the basket-maker all the year round. Sometimes, however, the willows are merely left to stand in water after grading until May, June, or July instead of being boiled, or are cut when the sap is up in April or May, but these will be a white colour after peeling and can only be used from April until the end of June.

BASKET-MAKING

There are many varieties of willow—Black Mould, Champion Rod, Yellow Osier, Black Spaniard and others—which the basket-maker uses, and he has numerous types of ware to make. His work would fit almost as well into the next chapter as here. On the commercial side he has to make fruit and vegetable baskets (probably his biggest line), sieves, strikes, cucumber flats, potato hampers (100), laundry baskets, crates, tradesmen's bicycle baskets, and many other articles, while for the home he also makes shopping, bicycle handlebar baskets, and women's work-baskets in huge quantities. Almost anything that is made of willow rods comes under him. Basket-making is a much maligned craft—probably because of the vast number of amateurs who, at one time, made inferior baskets of cane as a hobby. To give an idea of how little understanding many people have of the work, Mr. Gilbert Musgrave, who employs many craftsmen in the little Somerset village of Stoke St. Gregory, near Taunton, told me a good story recently. A visitor, after watching a group of craftsmen at work, expressed surprise that there was so much in it. He had thought that baskets were made by organ-grinders who travel round the country, complete with monkey, calling on householders and offering to grind their knives and make them a basket at the same time. As Mr. Musgrave points out, he has not been reduced to that yet! Nor indeed have any in his line, for basket-making is a job which not even the machine has yet been able to master.

The maker carefully selects his willows according to the type and size article he is to make. For a shopping variety, for instance, he takes lengths of 3, 4, and 5 feet which he soaks for a short time to render pliable and less liable to snap. Weaving his finer willows in and out of stouter ones, he first starts to make the bottom. He then lets in the stiff "uprights" and fastens them securely by working in several willows together to form the "upset." This is one of the hardest, yet most important stages, for it affects the whole strength of the finished basket. He now fills in the sides by weaving single willows (101)—a stage known as "randing"—and letting in occasional rows of several willows together—"slewing." When the sides are complete, he works his uprights back into them to form a neat border, and picks off all the short ends. The basket-maker, sitting on a floorboard with his back against the wall and his legs outstretched, weaving his basket on a lapboard with almost uncanny speed, is an interesting spectacle. His work has not changed greatly throughout the centuries (36), but cheap foreign imports from Germany, Holland, Belgium, and Poland nearly flooded him out before the war, when shopping baskets were imported and sold for as little as 1s. 6d. each. How could a craftsman, who takes a pride in his work, compete against such odds? With this competition removed, his work is appreciated again, after he had played a valuable part in the war effort. It is to be hoped that he will not be subjected to such unfair competition again when normal conditions return, for, though his prices may be higher than those of the Continent, his work is in a class on its own and, therefore, has a far longer life. The old slogan of the days of depression, "Buy British," applies here as well as anywhere. By supporting the English basket-maker we can help to give work and mental occupation to the wounded of both wars, who, unable to do many other forms of work, are being taught basket-making in the traditional style. Also, war conditions have proved that there is a place for women in the industry.

RUSH-WORK

Another kind of basket-work which, however, is now almost extinct in its traditional form but which is being revived as a handiwork, is the woven rush variety. It was in a basket of woven reeds that Moses was found in the bulrushes, and from earliest times loose rushes were used by all in place of carpets. Such work has been carried on traditionally in many parts until quite recent times. Still, I believe, rushes and sedge are cut and used for seating chairs or are woven into baskets and mats in the old style in a few areas of Somerset, Norfolk, Huntingdonshire, and Bedfordshire, while in other parts efforts are being made to revive the craft for the making of such articles as women's hats, church hassocks, needlework baskets, reseating chairs (102), and so on.

The rushes are gathered in mid or late summer by men in boats who wade into the water, and cut them below the surface, and then take them back to wash and dry in the shade for anything from 10 days to six weeks according to the method of drying adopted and the size of the rushes. For many forms of work, like the making of baskets and mats, the rushes are plaited. A pole is fixed horizontally along a wall, and one end of the rushes is tied to it. In this way several workers can plait their lengths at the same time, rolling the finished part back round the pole as they proceed. The lengths are later curled and twisted and sewn together into the required shapes and patterns.

In the old days they used to make horse-collars of rushes for breaking in difficult young colts. In some country districts lengths of rush were plaited together at each end and frayed in the centre by pulling them backwards and forwards over a metal comb attached to the edge of a table, odd pieces of rush then being bundled and let in to the frayed portion to form a soft padded section of greater thickness than the rest.

102. A SUSSEX BASKET-MAKER RE-SEATING A STOOL

103. SUSSEX TRUGS:
Shaving Panels by
Drawknife

104. SUSSEX TRUGS:
Making the
Framework

105. SUSSEX TRUGS:
Binding the Rim
round the Special
Frame

A 3-inch wide plait would be fastened round the outside and the ends were joined to form the shape of the collar.

Collars may still be made in this way in isolated areas, but I have never come across a craftsman who could do the work.

SUSSEX TRUGS

Entirely different from the osier basket is the Sussex trug, which derives its name from the old English "trog," meaning a shallow boat. The trugger's craft is one whose origin is in doubt. Many craftsmen to-day declare that the basket that we now know by that name was not made until about a century ago, yet there are mentions of trugs as far back as the 16th century. But, whatever its age, I do not believe it has ever been disputed reliably that the work was first started in Sussex or that it has remained essentially a county craft ever since, although why it has not spread to other parts is a mystery, for a better and more serviceable basket has yet to be made. It is favoured by farmers, fruit growers, and private gardeners alike, and it has even found popularity as far afield as California, to which country it has been exported from the Sussex countryside in quite large numbers.

The craft is carried on in only a few isolated areas of Sussex—chiefly at Hurstmonceux and East Hoathly—and the number of truggers is limited indeed. The trugger at work presents a picturesque sight as he sits at his "horse" shaving his strips, with bundles of finished baskets piled high around him, the floor of his shed strewn with wood shavings (103).

He starts by splitting his ash or chestnut rods and continues by steaming them for about 10 minutes in a quaint oblong wooden steamer before bending them through stakes into curves and then shaping them more drastically on a special rectangular wooden frame. The ends of the rods he nails together to form an oblong framework. Two of these frames he pushes through each other to intersect at right-angles before fastening them in the centre so that one frame forms the rim of the basket while the other makes a one-piece handle and base (104).

The trugger now cuts thin strips of willow and shaves them by draw-knife on his horse, shaping them into gentle curves slightly tapered at each end (103)—a most skilled operation. The middle of the strip is nailed to the centre of the base and the two ends are fastened to the rim. Further strips are fixed in similar way until the whole of the base is filled in, leaving only the handle part of the original framework showing (106). All that remains now is to trim the ends of the strips level with the rim.

The whole structure of the trug is designed for strength and fruit growers will show you baskets which they have used for years in almost as good condition as the day they left the craftsman's hand. Here is craftsmanship at its best, applied to a strictly utilitarian article. The work is not learnt in a day, nor can it be hurried. It takes years before a man is really good at the craft, and even then he is a fast worker if he can make more than about 50 trugs in a week. No one would deny that the trug is graceful, yet its grace is not intentional; it has come naturally in the true sense of craftsmanship.

There is a good story—for which I cannot vouch—about the way an early craftsman tried to popularise the trug. A number of Sussex yokels, it is said, were drinking merrily in a village "pub" one night shortly before the Great Exhibition of 1851, when one of them, amid much laughter, suggested that even the old trug might find its way there. His suggestion was taken up seriously by a trugger present, who walked to London and back to arrange for a display of the baskets. Since then the demand has always been greater than the supply. There is still plenty of scope for development. Some enterprising craftsman from another part might do well to make a similar journey—though not necessarily on foot—to Sussex to learn the secrets of the work, and thus spread the industry. It would be worth it.

LADDER-MAKING

It is not so long since ladders were made almost entirely in the woods or in the wheelwright's yard. Now, they are mostly mass-produced in the machine shop. Even so, the hand-made article remains the best, and is still favoured by the thatcher and other craftsmen who have every reason to appreciate more than others the superior quality.

While some wheelwrights still do this work, there are also a few ladder-makers to be found in rural areas. Unlike the machine shop, who in normal times import their poles from Russia or the Scandinavian countries, the hand workers have their larch or spruce cut in the neighbouring woodlands. When the poles are well seasoned they cleave or saw them into two sections of equal thickness, each having one side flat and the other rounded. Resting his poles together on shallow supports, just clear of the ground with the rounded sides downwards,

106. SUSSEX TRUGS:
A Craftsman Nailing
on the Final Panel

107. LADDER-
MAKING:
Gauging the cir-
cumference of the
Ends of the Rungs

108. LADDER-
MAKING:
Knocking the
Rungs into the
Poles

109. LADDER-
MAKING:
Trimming up a
Handmade Ladder

the ladder-maker evens up the flat sides with plane or draw-knife, and spaces out the positions for his rungs before boring the holes 9 inches apart with his auger. The rungs he cuts to various lengths and shapes at his horse with draw-knife or spokeshave. With almost uncanny precision the craftsman will make all his rungs of almost uniform size, simply by judgment. Each rung must fit tightly into the poles, however, so that the ends must be shaped and cut to an exact fit (108). To help him in this, he uses a shallow wooden gauge into which he knocks each end of his rungs in turn as a test for size (107). A secure fit in the gauge will mean an equally firm one in the ladder-poles.

The rungs are knocked into one section of the pole (108) and the second section is laid over the other ends of the rungs before the whole is hammered securely into position. The ladder is now cramped up for the poles to be trimmed by draw-knife (109) or plane and, to give extra strength, metal rungs are fastened through at intervals. Ladders are made to any size required. The average ranges from 15 to 30 feet, but one craftsman told me of a "real whopper" of 50 feet he once made.

HAY-RAKES

Like ladders, hay-rakes are now made mostly by machinery, but they too are still hand-made in quite large numbers by small bands of craftsmen in odd country districts. These bands—generally numbering only two or three men and an apprentice—also undertake the making of such articles as hen-coops, pump-buckets, sheep-cribs, tool-handles, mole-traps, and many other utensils for land work. They work in yards and small sheds equipped with hand tools, and perhaps a lathe. In effect they are specialist carpenters who fit their work according to the demands of the season. Their work is of a high standard, and they carry it out at a remarkable speed. At one such centre, for instance, I was told that the three of them make as many as 4,000 hay-rakes by hand every season and the making of a rake is a long and highly skilled business.

From the time the ash is felled and rinded, it is well over a year before the finishing touches can be given to a rake, and it will have gone through many stages during that time. After lengthy seasoning, the straighter poles are selected and are roughly hewn by axe into handles. If necessary, they are straightened by steam before being fixed in the "horse," and shaped and trimmed by draw-knife until of fairly even thickness (112). Next, one end is held taut in a wall-vice, while the

K

other end is passed through a circular plane which is swivelled down the entire length (113), shaving it on its course into a clean even surface throughout. Some workers turn the handles on the lathe, but there are many who still swear by the old method. One end of the handle is split downwards to a depth of about 18 inches to form the prongs for fitting to the head, and a metal band is fastened round the base of the cut to prevent further splitting. In the case of a drag-rake, the split is made for the greater length of the handle, a V-shaped wedge is driven into the fork, and two sections of turned wood are inserted beyond the wedge to allow easier handling in the hay-field and to give extra strength.

Shorter poles are now cut and roughly trimmed for the heads, holes are bored for the teeth, and the head is squared, evened up, and trimmed afresh—again by means of draw-knife (110) and horse. Although the lathe is used by many for turning the teeth, these are still made in a most primitive way in some yards. Short pegs—about twice the length of the finished tooth—are driven into a small metal cylinder—one at a time—the diameter of which is considerably less than the thickness of the pegs. The driving force of the mallet rams the peg down into the cylinder in such a way that its sides penetrate down the length of the peg, cutting it into exactly the right size and shape of a tooth, the surplus wood peeling off like an apple-skin. The peg is then lifted out and the tooth portion is cut off and tapered at one end. The rake head is now held firmly in a vice and the tapered ends are driven into the holes (111). When all are in place the teeth are pointed and the handle is fixed to the head by forcing the prongs into two holes drilled in the shoulder of the head and securing by screws (114).

THE COOPER

Before many more years have elapsed the cooper, who has worked traditionally in the English countryside for some 2,000 years (2), is likely to have died out completely, as more and more of the articles he once made so beautifully are turned out by machinery or are superseded by galvanised ware.

Modern conditions grow to justify less and less those patient hours he spends cleaving his oak or teak and shaping his staves by special curved planes—some 5 feet in length—or else by knives, as in earlier times, so that they are wider in the centre than at the ends. It is skilled

110. HAY RAKES:
Squaring up the
Rake Head by
Draw-knife

111. HAY RAKES:
Fixing the Teeth
to the Rake Head

112. HAY RAKES:
Making the
Handles

113. HAY RAKES:
Smoothing the
Rake Handle by a
Special Circular
Plane

work, indeed, fixing the well-soaked staves together by bending them in front of a fire into the gentle curves of a barrel, and driving truss-hoops of various sizes over them, taking care always to see that they are tightly wedged to give a firm fit such as will render the finished barrel watertight. No less difficult is the cutting out and bevelling of the head by curved knife, or the grooving of the inside into which the head will later be fitted.

It is something of a rarity to find a craftsman doing this work now. Such men only exist in a few areas where there is a special local demand for the better type of hand work. But for centuries the cooper was a craftsman upon whom many depended in some way. The barrels for the fish markets were his product. He made the wooden tubs for the stables and for carrying food for poultry and other livestock; he served the needs of the cheese-makers of Cheshire, and he supplied the hoppers of Kent with barrels for their beer and the Devon farmers with casks for their cider. He made, too, most of the utensils—churns, butter-casks, tubs, and so on—for the dairy. In short, he made in wood the greater number of articles for everyday farm and domestic use such as are now mass-produced in galvanised form.

GLOVE-MAKING

Although Somerset is regarded as the principal centre of the glover, agricultural gloves are made in quite a number of parts—especially in areas where there is a local tannery—by both men and women.

There are not many stages in the craft but, like all forms of hand work, it is skilled. As one hedger once put it to me as he pulled away some vicious-looking undergrowth, "the glove is our first line of defence," and anyone who has seen a hedger at work, and realises the kind of thing he is up against, will get his meaning.

Skins which have been cured but not tanned are carefully cut out to pattern in duplicate by means of a sharp knife. The finger-space is left as a single piece, but a separate section is cut away for the thumb. Holes are punched round the edge, and the two skins are then sewn together with a leather thong. Where possible, the hedger will get the glover to make his gloves specially for him, as the better the fit the less likely are his hands to blister when he works.

Teazle-knapping

Although hardly a craft in itself, teazle-knapping is carried out in a few areas of Somerset and Devon for the benefit of the weavers, who need teazle heads to raise the nap of their cloths.

The teazle plants are mainly cultivated by women, who go out head-harvesting with special gloves and short curved knives in July or August, well armed against the prickly leaves and stems. Each plant yields anything up to 100 heads, and these are dried in the sun, and done up in packets containing about 20,000 each before being sent to the weavers and to the cloth mills. A teazle plantation is useless for seven years after harvesting, yet the heads are badly needed by cloth manufacturers and the demand far exceeds the supply.

VIII

COTTAGE AND HOME CRAFTS

In olden days when communications in the country were bad, and it was something of an adventure and just a little "dashing" to travel more than 5 or 10 miles out of the village, and when forms of entertainment were few and far between, villagers put their leisure hours to useful purposes. One of their chief pleasures lay in doing some form of hand work in their cottages. The womenfolk might make lace or quilts at odd moments during the day and again in the evening, while the men would settle down to making straw bee-skeps or toys for the children, or to making "treen" when they returned home, weary after a day's work in the fields. Some would spend their time travelling round the district as tinkers, riveting china, as indeed they still do (115).

To the cottagers it was not work but a pleasant way of passing what would otherwise have been long idle hours, and it enabled them to make a little extra money too, which must have been welcome in days of such bad wages. Of course, the pay for their hand work was more often than not extremely poor, and obviously did not justify those long hours of care and patience, but, from the cottagers' point of view, it was payment for a hobby, and well worth while. They turned out excellent work simply for the love of it, and many fine crafts were thus born in England's cottage homes.

Some of these crafts have died out and been forgotten long ago; others still survive feebly, but are worth preserving where they yet have their uses: while a few have developed considerably. Crafts like toy-making have become a whole-time work, carried out by hand craftsmen in small village workshops, and the development of sport on the village green has led to another craft for the home—the making of cricket-bats. When the little Hampshire village of Hambledon first put cricket on the map it gave birth at the same time to a craft that has developed from little more than a cottage industry into one with a world-wide export.

LACE-MAKING

It was the persecution by Philip II of Spain in the Low Countries during the 16th century that is popularly supposed to have led to the start of the lace-making craft, one of our most beautiful cottage industries. Flemish protestants fled from Mechlin and settled in the Bedfordshire village of Cranfield, only to be joined a few years later by Huguenots from Lille, who made their homes in many parts of England. The refugees made various types of lace, and they lost no time in passing on the secrets to the villagers, so that by the 17th century lace had gained fame and had become fashionable among Royalty no less than among others of the aristocracy. Districts such as Honiton and Beer in Devon, Ripon in Yorkshire, and parts of Norfolk, Bedfordshire, and Buckinghamshire developed their individual styles which, in some cases, have been handed down traditionally (21) ever since until now there are the point-ground in Buckinghamshire; the Maltese, torchon, and Cluny in Bedfordshire; and the Honiton pillow-lace in parts of Devon (116, 117). Here it is interesting to note that although Honiton is the name given to Devon lace, it is really misleading. Most of the lace has always been made in other parts of the county and it gets its name merely because Honiton has been the central clearing-point for the transport of the lace to London.

Lace schools were started in many parts, and for a time the craft was more than a hobby, even though it was always carried on mainly in the home with, perhaps, a lace shop in the village. Lace became the rage, and it mattered far more that a child should be able to make a good piece than that she should be able to read or write. Children were taught the work as young as 5, and in one or two parts harsh punishments have been recorded, such as rubbing their noses on the heads of the pins if they did not learn sufficiently quickly.

It can have been no easy work for a child and, judging by the intricacies of the craft, few can have learnt more than the simple stitches. The making of the initial design in itself is often so difficult that few lacemakers, and certainly no one without a very sound knowledge of the working of the bobbins, can ever undertake it. The design is drawn on to white cardboard and then pricked through on to brown pasteboard, the outline made by the pinholes being joined up by ink-lines in the case of Buckinghamshire lace. This might be simple enough if it was not

114. HAY RAKES:
Fixing the
Rake Handle

115. THE TINKER:
A country China Riveter at work

116. LACE-
MAKING:
Children
Learning
Honiton style
in Devon

117. LACE-MAKING:
Showing the Special
Straw-stuffed
Pillow and the
Bobbins

so easy to design a pattern which it is quite impossible to work with the bobbins!

It would take a really competent lace-maker to describe her complicated craft in any detail, and even then it is doubtful how many would really be much the wiser. The general principle, however, is that linen thread is wound on to bobbins, and the pattern is pinned on to a special straw-stuffed pillow, with the bobbins suspended all round it (117). The pillow is set on a stool or low table in front of the worker, and the lace is made by moving the bobbins in such a way as to work the thread in and out of the pins to form the required pattern. It looks so easy when you see a gifted worker moving her bobbins at a speed that would make even a fast knitter marvel, but I need hardly say that this is only a deception. The beauty of lace is too well known for anyone to imagine that the making of it could be easy.

Lace made in the English cottage homes has been sent all over the world and has long been popular with Royalty. Tradition has it that Catherine of Aragon once did much to help the industry in Bedfordshire, but I find this unconvincing as dates are difficult to fit in. Yet it was a Devon lace-designer, Miss Jane Bidney, who, in 1840, collected together 100 of the best lace-makers in the county and made the lace for Queen Victoria's wedding-dress at a cost of £1,000. The Queen, it is said, was so delighted with the work that she commanded Miss Bidney to attend the wedding. A descendant of hers, Mrs. Ida Allen, can be found to-day at the lace shop at the little Devon fishing village of Beer. Mrs. Allen, too, is patronised by Royalty, and has made lace for the Queen, Queen Mary and the late Queen Alexandra. It is to her that Queen Mary sends much of her valuable old collection from time to time for reconditioning.

There is a world of tradition surrounding lace-making. Old patterns have been prized and handed down from generation to generation and are still worked by descendants of the early craftswomen. A deal of workmanship has gone into the making of some of the bobbins, too, for at one time it was the custom for suitors to have bobbins specially carved to present to their ladies; and there are customs like the "keeping of Cattern," when St. Catherine, the patron saint of spinners, is honoured by annual feasts and by the making of Cattern cakes.

Like many of our cottage crafts, lace-making has declined in recent years through changing fashions. Orders from America, where lace is still in favour, are helping to keep it alive in a few areas, but few girls are taking up the work and the craft is in danger of becoming all but extinct in some districts.

QUILTING

Ever since the 13th century—and possibly before that—women and young girls have made quilts in their homes in much the same way as the lace-makers. So traditional has been their craft that more and more details concerning its ancient origin and evolution have been lost with the passing of each succeeding generation of craftswomen who, caring little for written descriptions, left only their own and their ancestors' handiwork as a record of the industry.

From early inventories and manuscripts it appears that the women-folk first did the work to serve the needs of their own families, and that they probably did not start to sell it until the Middle Ages, when quilts were gaining popularity and were made, not only in the humble cottage homes, but also in the larger country houses. They found favour with Royalty too by the time of Henry VIII, for there are mentions of quilts in the Royal Wardrobe, while Charles I appears to have indirectly helped to raise the standard of the work by importing quilts from the East Indies, thereby introducing foreign influence.

In her *English Quilting*, Mrs. Elizabeth Hake, who a few years ago tried to trace back some of the history of the craft in Devon, maintains that quilting reached its height in technique and popularity in the 17th and 18th centuries, but declined again into a cottage industry in the following century when the "well-to-do" patronised the new mechani-cally woven materials.

Yet, in spite of the general decline, quilting is still carried on in the old style—mainly by elderly women—in parts of Northumberland and Durham and in many Welsh districts. These Quilt Wives are continuing the last traditional needlework left in England, and some of them are still working the same patterns as their Tudor ancestors.

The art of the quilter lies in stitching a layer of wool between two widths of material in such a way as to make attractive patterns of her stitches, while keeping her quilt even all over with her design standing out prominently in raised form. The beautiful, and often intricate, designs which she makes are the more remarkable because usually she has had no artistic training, and has learnt the work simply by word of mouth from her mother. Ask her to draw the most simple object and

118. HAND FABRIC
PRINTING:
Beating out the
Design

119. GLOVES MADE BY THE RINGWOOD HAND KNITTERS
Being Packed at the Depot

120. BEESKEPS:
William Hill,
the age of 8
at Camelsdale,
Surrey

121. BEESKEPS:
Making a Hole for the
Rod by means of a
Boxwood Peg

probably she cannot do it, yet she will sew her patterns s o that they are geometrically perfect. The secret is that the Quilt Wife composes her patterns from units. Objects such as feathers, hearts, chains, true-lovers' knots, roses, leaves, and many others are traced on to stiff cardboard to form the required pattern of the various units, and are cut out as templates.

The Quilt Wife scours her wool and cards it in much the same way as the spinner, and then tacks each end of one of her widths of material to the webbing part of the two adjustable rollers of her quilting-frame and sets it taut. Next she sews one end of her other width to the webbing, and spreads her wool evenly over the first piece before drawing the second width over the wool and fixing this taut to the other end. Then, laying her template over the top width, she scratches or chalks her outline.

Working from either the corners or the centre, she now stitches along her outlines to produce the quilted effect. When making a large object, such as a bed-quilt, she works in sections, winding the finished portion off on to one of the rollers of her frame, and unwinding a similar amount of material from the other roller—taking care that the new section is as taut as the first.

The quilter can get infinite variety into her work by her choice of design, and she can make beautiful articles out of scrap. What more attractive than the old-world patchwork quilt, where the top material comprised odd pieces of chintz curtains or women's dresses, sewn together into one piece? Sometimes the Quilt Wife would choose to stitch along her patches; at others she would ignore them entirely and make a further design as if she were working on plain material.

The secret of craftsmanship—the combination of usefulness with beauty—is to be found as much in her work as in the manual crafts. The main object of quilting is to provide warmth with lightness, and all the stitching is done with the object of keeping the wool padding evenly distributed between the two widths of material. The fact that the resultant raised effect is more often than not delightful is really incidental. The craftswoman arranges her stitching lines in the form of designs because she likes to make them as attractive as possible while she is about it, but every stitch she sews is necessary and not frivolous.

Through the offices of the Women's Institute and the Rural Industries Bureau, attempts are being made to revive this fine old craft. May they be successful, for quilting still has a useful part to play in the way of

L

providing soft furnishings and various types of women's clothing. And while the work is maintained in the traditional style it will continue to be as appropriate to the 20th century as to Tudor times.

HAND FABRIC-PRINTING

Like many other crafts, fabric-printing by hand is practically dead, and what is left of it is really more of a town than a country craft now. It was once practised in the larger country homes, however, and it is still carried on by a few women in various rural districts.

In olden times the women would print their own dress lengths in this way, and some of the most attractive chintzes, such as adorned the windows of old cottages, were "beaten off" at home by the women-folk. Although the craft was practised by the Egyptians and the Chinese some 2,000 years ago, it did not reach Europe until the 11th century, when monks made wood blocks and printed textiles along the banks of the Rhine, and it does not appear to have found its way to England until the end of the 17th century, when a refugee from France opened the first print-works at Richmond in Surrey.

With materials printed so cheaply by machinery these days, there are comparatively few women left who know the secrets of the work, but the war caused more to take it up. It is a tribute to hand work that many fashion-designers are now learning the craft in an effort to help them improve the standard of their work and thus enable them to take a more prominent lead in the world's fashion market. As with weaving, so there is now a greater leaning to the view that this hand craft should form the basis of good design.

In many respects the craft is similar to the old woodcut method of printing on paper. Blocks are carefully made in three pieces, which are glued together and jointed for strength. The design is first drawn and painted on paper and is then traced on to the block, which is cut by means of chisels, gouges, and special knives, the lines of the pattern being cut at an angle in such a way that they stand up in the form of an inverted V. The waste wood is scooped out and the lines are left with a firm base, such as will allow them to stand up well to the hard beating when printing takes place.

The block is "flocked" by coating it with a mordant and sprinkling on flocking-powder. When it is dry the process is repeated, and the outline is trimmed up with a sharp knife. Many women make their own dye,

122. BEESKEPS:
Making the
Bottom

123. NEW FOREST
TOYS:
Mr. Whittington
Assembling a
Model made in
his workshop

124. NEW FOREST
TOYS:
Carving behind th
ears of a pony

125. NEW FOREST
TOYS:
Some of the Models
being Inspected be-
fore Painting

which they apply by brushing it on to a special dye-sieve, and then running a squeegee first over the sieve and then over the block.

The material is held taut over a table and the block is laid face downwards on it and beaten with a mallet (118), the greatest care being taken to ensure that after each beating the block is placed in exactly the right position to link up with the lines of the previous printing. It is a slow business, requiring careful attention, for unless the mallet is worked evenly the colour will be patchy. Each colour needs a separate block, so that the craftswoman working in more than one colour will often have to go over her design several times, beating out and carefully linking up fresh patterns into the middle of her original one. A Dorset woman once told me that it takes her half an hour to beat out quite a short length of narrow material in only two colours.

After printing the fabric is rolled in mackintosh and dry steamed, fixed by the aid of a solution of salts, washed, and dried.

RINGWOOD HAND-KNIT GLOVES

Knitting is far too general a work to be regarded any longer as a craft in the true sense, yet mention must be made of the Ringwood glove-knitters, for they constitute what is probably the last cottage industry of the kind in England, and their work goes all over the world.

First started over a century ago, there are now about 800 women in the industry. Comparatively few of them know each other, yet all have one thing in common—they work to a stitch of their own which is not to be found in any book, and of which no one who has not had some connection with Ringwood has ever heard. The industry began when a number of Ringwood folk got together and invented their special "patent." For years the work was only done in Ringwood but, as the local lasses married and went away, the industry spread, until now the workers are to be found scattered all over England. To some of them this little Hampshire town is but a name. They only know the stitch because it has been handed down to them by their ancestors. But the local tradition remains, for the present workers keep faith. Each is sent her wool from Ringwood, and this she knits up into gloves at home in the traditional way, returning the finished articles to a central depot (119). In many cases the women like to keep the work as a link with their old home-town, and will travel many miles to hand in their gloves rather than post them.

I do not know the secret of their stitch, and if I did I could not tell it or I should be breaking faith. What I do know is that the gloves have a popularity of their own, and hold a wide market. This little industry has played its part in many wars, too. Its workers made gloves for the soldiers of Crimea, and in the Second Great War they made many thousands of pairs for the Services. The women knit an average of something like 3,000 pairs a week and the greater number of them are getting on in years, some being over 80.

STRAW BEE-SKEPS

The cottager and his bees have long been a traditional feature of the countryside. No village home was complete without a skep or two in the orchard, and there are many superstitions in being to this day connected with bees. In some parts cottagers still make it their first duty to go out and inform the bees of a death in the house, walking three times round the skeps and tapping on each with the words, "Father's dead."

Bee-keeping has lost none of its popularity, but the old-fashioned skeps have long ago given place almost entirely to the modern, and admittedly more luxurious, wooden hives. Fortunately, there are still to be found in parts of Surrey, Hertfordshire, and Sussex a few people who remain faithful to the skep. Thus only does one of the most picturesque of country crafts survive.

The skep-maker at work outside his cottage door on a summer evening was once a familiar sight. There was something peaceful and leisurely about his work, which is probably one of the reasons why it was usually carried on in the evenings by men who had toiled in the fields and woodlands all day. Typical of their kind was William Hill, who was still making skeps up to the time of his death a short while ago at the age of 86 (120-122). He had been making skeps ever since he was 9 and, as he sat on his upturned beer-barrel outside his cottage door in the peaceful Surrey village of Camelsdale, the evening sun glistening on his stubbly beard and side-whiskers, his curved pipe dangling from his mouth, it was hard to believe that he was not really living in a bygone age.

William once told me that when he was a boy his was a truly traditional craft. You were never taught it in the true sense of teaching, you just learnt it. To the average village child it was an entertainment to sit watching a bee-skep maker at work and, as time went on, to be allowed to try such jobs as splitting some of the boughs. Thus he would learn his craft in childhood—simply by watching. William learnt by watching an old woman in his village. But, unhappily, William also admitted that those days are gone. He knew no other craftsman of his kind, although recently he had had many requests to teach the work to younger men, for the war had caused an increasing demand for the skep again.

Hazel-boughs and wheat-straws are the most favoured materials for the work, although in some areas willows are preferred. The hazel is cut before the sap runs to prevent brittleness, only rods which are not likely to crack or snap being selected. The rods are split with a sharp knife, the necessary fineness making this both delicate and tricky. The finer the splitting the better, for each strand—known as the "split"—is used for binding the straw. Each stick should split into at least four strands. The straw, too, has to be carefully chosen—only long strands being suitable—and the day before it is to be used it must be slightly damped.

To start the skep, strands of straw are bound together with a split and wound round a small circular block of wood to which the whole is then nailed. This will eventually form the centre of the top (122). For circle after circle the split is bound over and round the straw—which must be constantly "fed" with fresh handfuls—and threaded through the previous row, each row becoming slightly larger in circumference than the one before. After a few rows a slight pulling pressure is exerted on the straw—thus bringing about the dome shape—the pressure increasing later to start the sides. So tightly must the craftsman bind his straw that he has to make a hole with a boxwood peg before he can push his split through it (121). When the last circle of the skep is finished the end rows are nailed to a wooden hoop in one part of which a slot has been cut to form a doorway for the bees.

A craftsman once told me that he can remember the days when he considered a shilling satisfactory payment for a skep, yet I have heard of them fetching as much as 10s. each in recent times.

BEEHIVE WORK

In the old days many other types of straw-work were carried out on the same lines. There were fruit and potato baskets or tubs, straw beds for shepherds to use in the lambing season, chairs for cottage homes, and many other articles, most of them useful, but a few merely ornamental. The work, known as beehive work, is simply a variety of skep-making, the general principles of binding straw with hazel or willow rods underlying each.

The number of articles made in this way now is limited. The potato tub is still made occasionally and, although I have never seen it done myself, I believe that in a few remote country districts shepherds still make their lambing beds on beehive lines.

TOY-MAKING

The children of primitive man needed amusing as much as those of our own time, and the men and women of those early days undoubtedly devised games and toys of a sort for their benefit. Many of the toys were made of wood and have, therefore, perished long since so that it is impossible to tell exactly how or when they were first made in this country.

The Quennells, in their *History of Everyday Things in England* volumes, trace the doll back at least to the start of St. Bartholomew's Fair in 1133, and they quote interesting cases of toy soldiers operated by strings being made about the same time. But already toy-making had reached such a high standard of both workmanship and enterprise that it is obvious that it had even then become a well-established craft which must have found its origin many centuries earlier.

As a child will often take more notice of an empty match-box than of an expensive toy, caring little about the hours of workmanship that have gone into its making, it is typical of the craftsman that he should have taken almost as much trouble over the making of a toy as over a piece of furniture. Some of the models that have been handed down to us reveal a masterly standard. Such craftsmanship in toys has long ago vanished, and instead machine-made ones now find their way on to the market which are often little more than a swindle. Many of the best toys are made these days by amateur carpenters, but, here and there, you will occasionally come across a hand toy-maker of the right type. One of the most interesting examples is to be found at Brockenhurst, in the heart of the New Forest, where artists and craftsmen are combining to produce elaborate, and really exquisite, models of animals. This is one of the few—very few—examples of how the Arts and Crafts movement *might* have succeeded. There is nothing "arty" about making his own bat. The success of his experiment can be seen by the fact that within six years he had abandoned most of his former trade to make bats whole-time. Since then bats have been made by hand here for many Test cricketers, including W. G. Grace, "Ranji," Fry, and Hammond. In the workshop can still be seen a letter from "W.G." relating how he scored his 100th century and his 1,000 runs for May with one of Mr. Nicolls's bats.

Locally grown and Essex willows are used, an average tree making about 36 bats, although one of the older men, who told me with pride that he had made as many as 50,000 bats in his time, recalls a "real giant" that yielded 300.

These willows are grown from "sets," great care being taken in their choice and in the tending of them when young. With suitable treatment a tree should have reached a circumference of 50 inches, five feet from the ground, after 12 years, and will then be ready for felling, a stage which takes place in winter when the willows are sawn into rounds 28 inches long. These rounds are split into clefts in such a way that the finished blade always follows the natural grain of the wood, and are then taken indoors and sawn into shapes very roughly resembling bats. After grading, they are stacked "criss-cross" out of doors (127) to season for about 9 months before being re-stacked in drying-sheds for a further 3 months. It thus takes more than a year to carry out the pre-liminary stages of the craft.

The faces and edges are roughly shaped, and the blade is passed through a quaint kind of press, designed to harden the surface to avoid scarring when the bat comes into contact with the hard ball. This is done by passing the blade upwards and downwards between two hand-turned rollers which give a pressure of 2 tons to the square inch. Afterwards, the edges are hammered to make them more durable, and the blades are sawn into their correct lengths. By means of a draw-knife the craftsman now roughly shapes the backs of the blades before passing them on for the splices to be cut on the circular saw, after which they are ready for the handles to be let in.

The handles are made from cane from the East Indies, where it grows to extraordinary lengths like a creeper. It takes two men to lift one of these bundles and carry it to the workshop (128), where it is sawn into handle lengths and planed into rounds, which are glued together to form "slips" (129), which, in turn, are later glued together and shaped by draw-knife into handles, each of which comprises anything from their work—just a true reproduction of Nature in a way useful to craftsmanship.

Mr. F. H. Whittington (123), an artist of wide experience, devotes his time to sketching and painting animals from life, spending hours wandering in the Forest catching the famous ponies in their various attitudes, visiting farms, and so on. Working from his beautiful coloured sketches, craftsmen then cut out and carve minutely detailed models in wood (124). Altogether they have made models of more than 200 different kinds of animals. Each is carved to scale, and represents a true reproduction in miniature of the actual animal, which is later painted in the correct colourings by another artist (126). Nor is the work confined solely to animals. Mr. Whittington and his workers also turn out, in similar style, models of coaches and postilions (123), and they aspire beyond toys to the making of church cribs with equal skill.

Here the value of the handcraftsman is well illustrated, for the toys are so unique that they are exported widely to the United States and to the Dominions, thus helping the dollar exchange. Here, too, is a case of modern craftsmanship, without family tradition, succeeding—a happy augury for the future. There is plenty of scope for development on these lines, and Mr. Whittington is doing his best to spread the spirit of craftsmanship by training, in his spare time, young boys and girls in the Hampshire villages to take up such work.

Making Cricket-bats

From toys to cricket-bats may seem a long step, yet both are for home entertainment. By comparison with toys generally, the making of cricket-bats by hand is a modern craft, but it has few equals for skill, and it undoubtedly has a future. The work is carried out in only a few areas, such as Sussex, Cambridgeshire, Nottinghamshire, and parts of Yorkshire. In each of these districts bands of craftsmen are to be found working daily making bats in huge quantities for use, not only by leading Test and county cricketers and by schools and universities, but also for export to Australia, South Africa, New Zealand, and the West Indies. During the war they were made largely for the Forces.

In the little Sussex village of Robertsbridge, one of the oldest centres, the craft was started as recently as 1870, when the village carpenter, Mr. L. J. Nicolls, himself a keen cricketer, decided to try his hand at

128. CRICKET BATS
It takes two m[e]
to carry a bun[d]
of Handle Cane
the Workshop

129. CRICKET BATS:
Glueing Strips of
Cane together for
the Handle

126. NEW FOREST
TOYS:
An Artist Painting
the Models in their
natural colours

127.   CRICKET BATS:
Stacking the Blades
for Open Air
Seasoning

130. CRICKET BATS:
Cramping up the
Bat Handles to Set

131. CRICKET BATS:
Shaping the
Handles

132. A BOATMAN PAINTING HIS CRAFT

133. CORACLE-MAKING IN WALES

12 to 16 pieces of cane. Between the slips pieces of rubber (the springing) are let in to prevent jarring on the batsman's hand and the finished handles are cramped up in a special rack to set (130).

Next comes one of the most intricate stages of the craft—fitting the handles to the bat. Only a critically sharp tool and finest degree of accuracy with the plane on the "tooth" of the handle will ensure a perfect fit, and a bad fit means a useless bat. The bat is now "built" and ready for the final shaping of the face, back, bottom, shoulders, and handle (131), all of which is done by either plane or spokeshave. Only the most accomplished craftsman can attempt these finishing stages, as each blade must be treated individually and have exactly the right amount of wood left to ensure a perfect balance. One shave too much can completely upset a balance, and cricketers are very particular about this point. The finished bat is passed over a sanding belt and burnished and the handles are strung by means of a kind of lathe.

"TREEN"

Long before pewter or silver came into general use, everyday domestic utensils were made of wood. They made "treen" at Glastonbury, and articles of turned wood were undoubtedly the first to be made as alternatives to pottery.

Almost from the start, the making of treen has been a cottage industry. The menfolk would fit up a workshop in their home, or build a shed in the garden, which they would equip with an old pole-lathe. They would have their queer-shaped chisels forged by the village blacksmith, and in these quaint little workshops they would work in the evening turning all kinds of bowls for family use. At first they did the work of necessity, knowing that otherwise their homes would lack many sorely needed articles. It was a case of "make it yourself or go without." The more highly skilled naturally took to the work better than the others, and they devoted long hours to the craft, turning out far more articles than they needed and selling them to the richer classes, who were in just as much need of them, but who, as yet, had no thought of doing any work themselves if they could possibly get it done by others.

At first the cottagers made chiefly bowls for drinking out of or for storing liquids, but in course of time they became highly efficient workmen, covering a wide field, until by Elizabethan times they had

M

learnt the art of choosing their wood in such a way as to make the grain play an important part in the finished appearance. They now added silver bands to their maple drinking-vessels, and in the Middle Ages they turned elaborate wassailing cups for containing hot punch. A keen rivalry existed in most villages to see who could turn the best bowl, and the maiden daughters of these craftsmen would deck them with ribbons and rosemary and carry them through the village streets singing carols at Christmas.

Whatever he made, the turner delighted to get individuality into his work. He fashioned wooden tankards with hinged lids, letting a pegged scale of quantities into the inside so that a customer ordering his drink could move his peg according to the quantity he required. (Incidentally, it is from this fashion that the expressions of "knocking back a peg" and "taking down a peg" are derived.) Many and varied were his styles of tankard, some plain and simple, but others intricately carved and shaped. He made, too, the wooden platters in the days when table manners were yet to be learnt. The food was brought to table in huge wooden bowls of his making and from these all would help themselves with their hands. Later, when manners were eventually discovered, these men fashioned knives, spoons, and forks as well.

The married men made useful articles of all kinds—coffee-mills, spice-boxes, butter-churns, candlesticks, cruet sets, apothecaries' mortars, and so on—but the young bachelors, with no homes of their own to worry about, spent much of their time turning knitting-sheaves, stay-busks, lace-bobbins, and other love-tokens for their maidens fair.

The development of the goldsmith and silversmith trades and the evolution of good pottery, china and glass caused a decline in the craft. The making of treen is now almost dead, but not quite so dead as many writers would have us believe. In recent months I have read no less than five descriptive articles about bowl-turners of the old school, and though they have all been about different craftsmen, each has described the worker as "the last exponent of the craft." The fact is that there are still a very few old-style bowl-turners in various parts. Mr. William Lailey, possibly the best-known of them, and certainly the most chronicled, may be the last of the Bucklebury treen-makers, but he is not the last in England as he has so often been described.

Except for one man who now uses a treadle-lathe, bowl-turners still remain faithful to the antiquated pole variety. They have their trees specially felled, and these they saw up into rectangular blocks, which they roughly shape by axe. They use special chisels, made by the local blacksmith, for cutting out their bowls as the blocks are revolved on the lathe. It is interesting to watch the dexterity with which they work. They actually make bowls from the insides of other bowls, for, after neatly hollowing out the inside of one, they proceed to make a second, and smaller, one from the block which they have just cut out.

There is an old-world atmosphere not only about their workshops but also about the work itself and sometimes about the workmen too. It is hard to imagine that one has not turned back a thousand years or more of English country life to see how men worked before the time of the Conqueror. The craft has changed so little since then.

Cider-making

Maybe it can hardly be called a craft in the strict sense, but cider-making is an interesting old country work—introduced, it is said, by the monks of Glastonbury—and is, I think, worthy of mention. There was, in fact, almost as much enthusiasm among the cider-makers of the 17th and 18th centuries over making a good product as existed among the craftsmen over fashioning a good article (32). Modern methods of processing and bottling have caused cider, as sold in most parts, to depreciate in taste, while the large firms now buy up the farmers' apples in such huge quantities that the old-style cider-making has almost died out. But it is still carried on in farms in Devon, Somerset, Dorset, Worcestershire, and Herefordshire.

The work is done in autumn or early winter when the apples are just beginning to show signs of rotting. Farmers have many ways of crushing their apples to pomace. In the past a huge millstone was turned by horse, but nowadays the crushing is mostly done by large grooved rollers, the juice and pulp being allowed to run into a tank. A Devon farmer told me quite recently, however, that in the southern part of his county many prefer to crush their apples through straw. They spread their apples out in rows in the press between layers of straw, pile them high, and leave them for some time to rot before clamping down the press to force the liquid into a wooden tub beneath. Whichever method is adopted, the liquid is left to ferment before being strained off into barrels.

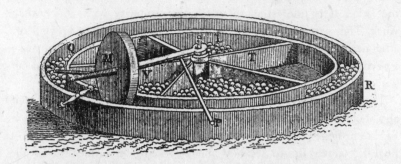

CIDER MILL, usually operated by a horse, whose collar is not shown.
Rather larger than the customary pattern

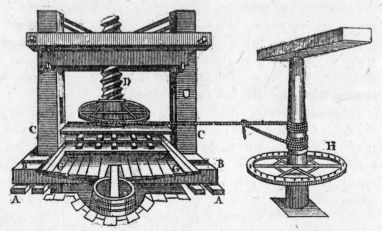

CIDER PRESS, operated by a rather unusual form of windlass gear

From engravings of 1793 by J. Halett

There is as much difference between the machine- and the home-made cider as between mass-produced and hand-made articles. If you doubt it, try a glass of each and judge for yourself. Then you will see why cider-making is regarded as a country craft.

IX

WATER CRAFTS

FROM the earliest times, when man first realised that a useful form of food was to be found in his streams and rivers, and so learnt to fish, and when he started to move about on water by means of log rafts, there have been crafts connected with both sea and river.

There were boat-builders of a kind thousands of years B.C., who made transport possible on water even before it had been developed to any extent on land; and there were those who made harpoons, traps, nets, and ropes for the men to catch their fish. Each one of our water crafts has steadily grown in importance during the intervening thousands of years until nearly all have now become mainly town industries.

But, although the shipwright's work has long been a vast organisation, employing thousands on the factory principle, village boat- and yacht-builders are yet to be found in the little coves around our shores. Most rope is made by machinery these days, but there are still a few old rope walks in use, and there are net-makers to be found who have been plying their craft since they were children. The hand sail-maker, I believe, has gone from the country entirely.

THE BOAT-BUILDER

Right back in the Early Stone Age men made boats. Doubtless, they started their work when they discovered—at the expense of many dippings—that logs had an unpleasant way of turning turtle unless they were shaped. Their first attempt to overcome this consisted of fastening together a number of logs to form a raft. Although this served many purposes, it was difficult to propel at any speed, and so they felled trees, hewed out the centres, and roughly shaped them. This was too strenuous work to justify the mediocre results, but it gave the boat-builder an idea, and it was not long before he was stripping the bark from gum trees with his axe and building efficient canoes. He cut down saplings to form the framework, and these he bent to shape and tied together with twigs at the ends. He shaped his bark by heating it over open fires until it was pliable. Then he would fasten the strips to his framework by tying grass ropes all round. Later he discovered that wattle work served his purpose better than saplings, and he also substituted hides for bark, lacing them together with leather thongs. He let in masts, too, and made sails of membrane.

Perhaps it was King Alfred who set the boat-builders working on any scale when he commanded long ships "taking 60 oars or more" to be built to oppose the esks. At any rate, by 1009 the boat-builder had become an important figure, using, it is said, over 300 hides to construct "massive vessels" for the newly formed navy which was now being built by levy.

Since those days the shipwright's work has steadily increased in importance until it has long been difficult to make a distinction between the "concern" and the individual. Throughout our long island history we have relied on him more than anyone for our national security and for our prosperity, for it is he who has always looked after our first line of defence. Where would Drake or Nelson have been without him, or how otherwise would we have had our export or import trades? Unlike many crafts, that of the shipwright has lost none of its glory or fine workmanship through development. Whether he works with only two or three others in small creeks or waterways, or whether he is but a unit in a large yard, that same skill is as apparent as ever.

The shipwright proper would fit better into a book on town crafts, but there are small bands of boat-builders who, I feel, must still be regarded as country craftsmen. If their methods are more orthodox to our way of thinking, they work in much the same spirit as their ancient ancestors. In their little yards and workshops—often only large enough to allow the construction of two rowing-boats at a time—set on the edge of the smaller harbours and coves around our shores, or by the bank of some river, they can be found working with all the skill of the wheelwright (133). Indeed, they need as much knowledge in the selection of their timber and choice of grain, while the attention they give to the shaping and fixing of their wood, in the making of both body and hull, must be no less careful.

Whether they are constructing a rowing-boat or yacht, or whether they are making a smack for the local fishing fleet, they know that men's lives depend on their work. Never will they use anything but the best seasoned timber, for they must not risk a shrinkage in the wood such as might cause a leak, and they will go to infinite pains to get the most perfect balance. The yacht, which has given such an impetus to their work in recent years, may give the greatest scope for design, but to the boat-builder the making of any kind of craft means good workmanship, and is, therefore, interesting to his way of thinking.

Many of these men are carrying on a tradition started by their ancestors hundreds of years ago—more often than not in the very same spots as they now work—until their very boats have assumed a family air, as each succeeding generation has introduced modifications of his own to meet changing needs. The mark of individuality is often so stamped that even an ordinary dinghy can be classified locally by a glance at its lines as the work of a certain family or band of craftsmen.

CORACLES

A first cousin to the hide-covered canoes of the Ancient Britons is to be found in the form of the coracle which has been made traditionally in Wales for well over 2,000 years. Men in the villages along the Towy, Wye, Teify, and Dee rivers can still be found making these strange floating baskets, weighing only about 10 pounds, and measuring some 5 or 6 feet in length and little more than a foot deep. They split and trim strips of ash by fromard and spokeshave, and weave their bands into position with well-soaked willows or hazel rods to form a framework. They let in a basket for the fish and a wooden seat—to which they attach a leather strap for carrying—and finish it off with a neat border in much the same way as the basket-maker. After the framework has been left to dry for a day or so in the sun, they cover it with calico or canvas, and tar it to render it waterproof.

Fishermen still use this strange craft for salmon fishing (133). Each man has his own coracle, and he walks from place to place carrying it on his back with only his feet and a small part of his legs showing. A comic sight, and surely the most primitive to be found in this 20th century! Two men set off together on their fishing expeditions, dragging a net between their coracles. They paddle with one hand and carry a wooden mallet with which to smite the salmon.

The coracle is not everybody's craft. I have never been in one, and I am not sure that I want to. It looks extremely dangerous, but the fisherman swears by it, and it is he who has to use it and not us—thank goodness! At any rate, it has survived in form longer than any other boat, so there must be something to commend it.

136. NET-MAKING:
Binding a Cork
to the Line

137. NET-MAKING:
Making a
Trammel

Rope- and Net-making

Ever since thousands of years ago men spun strands of coarse grass and intertwined them to make ropes for tree-climbing, men and women have been making ropes in England (20). They have been making nets of a kind, too, almost as long.

At least since the days of King John, Dorset in general, and Bridport in particular, have formed the principal centre for the industry. King John granted Bridport its charter "for the supplying of cordage to the King's navee," while both here and at Hamworthy, near by, ropes and nets were made for centuries for the Newfoundland fisheries. There are mentions of many Dorset flax mills in the Domesday Book, and these worked for both the rope- and sail-makers. In the museum at Stoke Abbot, according to *Dorset Up Along and Down Along*, an interesting historical booklet got out by members of the Dorset Federation of Women's Institutes, is to be found the old horn which, in later years, was blown at regular intervals to summon the flax-pullers to their drinks of cider.

Rope- and net-making are allied crafts. The net-maker uses the twine made by the roper, but, of course only a certain amount of his twine is made into nets. Although some men and women do both branches of the craft, most prefer to learn about each but to specialise in only one.

Both ropes and nets are now made mostly by machinery out of imported hemp or flax, but there are still a few hand-workers left who carry on both branches in the old style. In some of the smaller Dorset villages—of which Swyre is a notable example—and around Lowestoft and Yarmouth, women of all ages are to be found making nets of many kinds in their cottage homes in the same way as their families have been doing traditionally for centuries, and it is by no means unheard-of to find a woman of well over 70 who has been doing the work since early childhood. Right up to the middle of the last century nearly every fisherman made his own nets. Now, however, they mostly use machine-produced ones, and the hand-workers are only to be found to day at widely separated points along the south and east coasts. Although the number of ropers working in the old style is rapidly decreasing, there are a few in various parts of Essex, Derbyshire, and Yorkshire, and there are others at St. Ives in Huntingdonshire, at Yeovil, and at Hailsham in Sussex.

N

The work of the ropers and netters is manifold. They make cables and ropes for the Navy, for Trinity House, and for private seafarers, and they make halters for farmers and cord and string for sundry other uses. From their twine they weave all kinds of nets for the fishing fleets, camouflage-nets for military purposes, hammocks, life-saving nets, and tennis, football, and hockey nets for sports clubs.

Before the roper can make either cord or twine, he must hackle his hemp by repeatedly pulling skeins—which have already been scutted and retted—over a set of steel teeth attached to a bench until the fibres are straight and free of tangles. Then he spins his thread—a highly skilled stage which is seldom done by hand now. The roper winds his hemp round his waist and, after fastening a wisp to a hand-turned wheel, walks backwards, paying out the thread with his left hand and letting it run through his right hand, taking care to see that his threads turn evenly on each other. The machines now used for spinning work on exactly the same principle. The length he can make his rope is governed by the distance of his rope-walk. A few of the old walks stretch as far as a quarter of a mile, but the average is about 1,000 feet. After spinning, the lengths of the yarn are hardened, sized, and polished, and are twisted together into twine or rope. A number of strands are laid together and twisted round each other by means of two wheels, one of which twists the threads while the other tightens the twist.

Although the making of the twine in the first place is perhaps the most difficult part of the craft, the work of the net-maker is hardly less interesting. There are many varieties of fishing-net alone, and each requires a different-size twine, and has its peculiar stitch, while the needles, too, vary according to the mesh (134, 135).

The craftsman starts his net by winding his twine round a wooden mesh-gauge and knotting it up to form his foundation. This he hangs on a wall-hook, and then proceeds to make his net by threading his needle containing the twine over and under his loops in such a way that each is securely knotted at the same time. When a portion of the net has been woven, it is taken off the wall and hooked on to a board or table, the netter walking backwards as he works.

An old Devon netter told me that one of the hardest kinds to make is the trammel (137), used extensively for catching plaice, soles, dabs, brill, turbot, and other flatfish. For this he has to make three nets, one of smaller mesh than the other two. He threads a length of rope through a number of corks (137) and stretches it between two posts, and to this

38. MAKING CRAB-
POTS IN DEVON

139. MAKING CRAB-
POTS IN DEVON
Weaving the
Willows

140. LIME-BURNING

141. BRICKMAKING
BY HAND

he joins the three nets to make a triple thickness, with the finer one in the middle. He leaves the fine one slack so that, as the fish enter the net, their force will carry this net through one of the other two to form a pocket from which escape is impossible. The corks are designed to keep the head-line up, while a lead-line is passed through the bottom to keep the net down.

Whatever the net to be made, a high standard is set. The craftsman making a life-saver must never knot his twine, but must splice it for extra safety, and if a splice is made in the wrong place the whole net will be returned as bad work and unacceptable.

CRAB- AND LOBSTER-POTS

Few people, I suppose, other than those who live by the sea, have ever seen a crab- or lobster-pot being made, for, not only is it a seaside craft, but it is further restricted to the areas where such fishing takes place. Like many others, this craft has given place in some instances to quicker and more simple methods, such as the making of pots out of wire-netting. The wire soon rusts, however, and is in no way comparable to the old-fashioned willow pots. The old style remains the best, and fishermen can still be found plying the craft in many of the quaint little coves of south-west England and in the Welsh districts of Anglesey and Pembrokeshire.

The work is done almost entirely by men with a sound knowledge of this particular kind of fishing, for any fisherman will tell you that the size of his catch is governed largely by the shape and general soundness of his pot. The best pots are made of willows, as they will resist the tremendous pressure of water better than any other material. Unlike other types of basketry—and pot-making is really a form of basketry— the craftsman starts at the top and works downwards, or, to be more precise, he starts in the middle and works upwards and then downwards.

Taking anything from 8 to 12 stout canes as his uprights, he fixes these into holes in a circle of wood mounted on a stand, and proceeds to weave finer willows in and out of them to a height of about 9 inches. As he approaches this height he lets in more uprights and ends his weave. Leaving a space, he next plaits a number of strands through his willows, which he then bends slightly over and outwards (138, 139). A further space is left and the willows are stretched parallel with the ground while another row is plaited. After this, the willows are bent downwards while yet more rows are woven or plaited at intervals, the pot being finished off by threading the ends of the canes, after the final plaiting, through and into the preceding rows.

The pot can now be lifted from its stand, leaving sharp spikes of cane at the base of the uprights. Most makers leave these as they form an extra obstacle to trapped lobsters trying to escape. All that remains now is to fasten a brick to the inside to give extra weight, and to attach "corked" ropes. In normal seas a pot should last several seasons, and a skilled worker can turn out a pot in little over two hours.

EEL TRAPS

Rather different is the work of the eeltrap-maker, who is to be found working near the banks of rivers where eels abound, especially in the Fens. His craft is perhaps more individual than that of the crab-pot-maker, as each area has its favoured style. A maker will devise a trap which he will declare is more effective in his particular waters than any of the others, and thus, to a lesser extent, there exists that same local variety in eeltraps as is to be found in waggons.

In some parts craftsmen make long, pointed circular nets into which they let 4 or 5 small hoops at regular intervals, extending from one end to about half-way down the net; in other places the net is rejected, and willows, from which numerous styles can be made, are preferred. Setting a number of stout willows in a circular wooden block, known as an "eel chair," the craftsman proceeds to weave finer willows in and out in the same way as the basket-maker. Although fundamentally all work on the same principles, their finished articles differ enormously. Eels are by no means easy to catch, and the shapes have to be carefully worked out. They comprise a succession of curves and bends, narrow necks and bulges, and these can only be worked out by men with a thorough understanding of the habits of eels. In appearance, many are like Chinese lanterns. Perhaps they are based on them, for I once read that it was the Chinese who first introduced eel-fishing into England.

FISHING-RODS

Fishing has always been responsible for a number of crafts since the days of harpoons. While the net- and trap-makers have been busy from the start, and fish-hooks were made of flint in the Neolithic Age, the makers of fishing-rods do not appear to have really got going until about the 17th century, although by the 18th theirs was a highly specialised work. Some made entire rods; others preferred to specialise in certain branches of tackle.

Most fishing-rod and tackle makers appear to have been situated in London and other large towns, as is the case today, but much of the work was done for them by country craftsmen and, in many instances, they seem to have had little more to do than assemble the various parts and sell them.

X

SOME RURAL INDUSTRIES

BESIDES the more definite crafts we have examined, there are many
other interesting forms of country work that might perhaps be better
classified as rural industries. Many of them have long years of tradition
behind them, and all demand a high degree of workmanship and
enterprise.

Cornishmen have mined for tin since the time of the Phœnicians, and
they are doing so now on a greater scale than for many years since the
war caused a serious decline in our imports of this much needed metal.
The flint-knappers are still at work in Suffolk, and the hoppers are busy
in Kent. Lime-burning (140) is carried on in many parts, and there are
the paper-makers (13) in Devon, who make the treasury notes for the
Bank of England. Stone and marble are quarried in Dorset, and the
white pyramids round St. Austell stand testimony to the continuance of
the Cornish china-clay industry (142–145). Despite the mass-production
complex of so many builders, bricks are made by hand (141) in a number
of parts for the benefit of the few who still take a pride in their work.

PORTLAND AND PURBECK QUARRYMEN

Many of England's most famous buildings have been constructed of
stone or marble quarried by the men of Portland and Purbeck respec-
tively. After London had "burned like rotten sticks" in 1666, Sir
Christopher Wren used Portland stone for rebuilding the capital. Odd
pillars, said to have been chosen by him but for some reason or other
never used, can be seen by the quarries today. St. Paul's Cathedral
and many of the City churches were built of Portland stone, and in
more recent years the Cenotaph and much of Regent Street have been
added to the long records of this Dorset "isle." Marble, too, was sent
from Purbeck to be incorporated in the construction of Westminster
Abbey, the Tower of London, and in the cathedrals of Winchester,
Exeter, Salisbury, and Chichester. It too was greatly used in the rebuilding of London. The marble was shipped from Owre Quay, on Poole
Harbour, and the right-of-way to that spot is preserved today by kicking
a football along the road leading to it once a year.

142. CORNISH CHINA CLAY: A Pit Truck coming down the Railway set on the side of a pit

143. CORNISH CHINA CLAY: Bringing the China Clay into a Kiln

144. CORNISH
CHINA CLAY:
Looking down a
Clay Pit

145. CORNISH
CHINA CLAY:
Down a China
Clay Pit

But men quarried stone and marble at these places long before these times. Their work is so old that its origin is lost in antiquity, for the working of freestone was developed as far back as the Bronze Age. Some sovereign once granted the Purbeck quarrymen a charter, but which of them it was is not known. The original charter has long been lost—sold, it is said, by a previous Warden of the Quarrymen's Company in the days when the warden held the papers during his term of office and when attempts were being made to deprive the stone-workers of their rights and smash their power. There is a great tradition at Purbeck—a tradition that has kept men working at a high level. A man not descended from a quarryman has never been welcomed into this industry. Son would follow father for generations, and for centuries it was held that no boy who did not start in the quarries before he was 10 had any future. To this day, a man, on reaching the age of 21, pays an entrance fee of 6s. 8d. and buys a quart of beer and a small loaf of bread at the annual Shrovetide meeting of the company at Corfe Castle. Thus he becomes a member of the company and, while his name is being entered in the records, he watches one of the older men feast on his bread and beer. If he has been foolish enough to take the daughter of anyone but a quarryman for a wife before reaching 21, he must pay an extra 1s.!

A wealth of lore lingers round Portland, too. All stone exported from the common lands is liable to royalties at the rate of 1s. a ton. Half of this belongs to the King, but in 1665 Charles II rewarded the tenants for their loyalty during the Civil War by giving back part of his share, and the practice has been followed by sovereigns ever since.

At both centres there are men working with tools handed down to them through generations of their families. Only with long years of practice can a man become a good quarryman. The man of Purbeck requires a sound knowledge of his material and a deal of skill to excavate his marble in slabs of 6-inch thickness, the size most needed. In his *Purbeck Shop*, Eric Benfield, whose family have worked here for generations, says that a skilled craftsman should be able to judge a size to within a foot by the sound of his blows. Saws are not favoured at Purbeck, so the stone must be split with wedges and hammers, but it will only split in certain places, and it takes long practical experience to judge the "clifts"—spots where splitting is possible. And even if he has judged well, the craftsman must know just how to insert his wedges, and must gauge the force with which to wield his hammer according to the hardness of the particular piece he is working.

Anyone who doubts that there is skill in quarrying should visit these Dorset "isles." If the work seems slow at times it must be remembered that every blow with hammer or any other tool forms a carefully worked out feature of a long process, starting in Mother Earth and ending only when the builder puts the finishing touches to his building. The architecture of Wren would as surely have suffered if the quarrymen had lacked a real understanding of what was required of them as if the builders themselves had been bad. It was the perfect understanding between all three that prompted fine architecture, and it applied as much in the building of small parish churches and country houses as in the construction of large cathedrals. It was then that the builder was a craftsman. The stone is still there for the working, but when the rebuilding of Britain really gets into its stride, let it be used as much in the structural work of the country as of the towns and cities.

THE SLATERS

Men have quarried roofing slates since the days when the Roman used tiles or slats to roof their homes. The quarrying of slate is carried on traditionally today in parts of Derbyshire and Yorkshire, in the Cotswolds, and in the Lake District, and, more locally, round Horsham in Sussex, and at Collyweston, on the borders of Rutland and Northamptonshire, by men whose families have been plying the craft for centuries. Generally, they will give their slates a certain "social dignity" by naming them, according to size, from the "Queen" for the largest down—by way of the "princess," "duchess," "countess" and "viscountess"—to the "lady" for the smallest, but at Collyweston they prefer such names as "hautboy," "bachelor," "wivett," "middle-back," and so on.

The quarryman works at varying distances below ground. He "foxes" his stone by lying on his side and picking at the sand below the slate. As he proceeds to clear the sand to a depth of about 2 feet, he runs stout props under the slate to prevent premature subsidence. Not until a faint cracking sound is heard—imperceptible to the normal being—does he stop his picking. Then the props are systematically removed, and the slate is allowed to crash down, breaking up into large slabs which can be levered up and roughly broken by hammer into "logs."

These logs are taken to the surface and laid out on the "patch," and it is here that the craftsman works with Nature in much the same way as the woodman. He waters his logs regularly, and relies on Jack Frost to carry out the next stage. The water percolates into the soft "veins" of the slate and, when it freezes, the tremendous force of expansion splits open the slate into neat regular layers. When Nature has played her part, the slater takes his slabs to his strange little improvised workshop, built of straw and laths, where, sitting on a stool with his slate standing on edge in front of him, he "clives" his layers by chopping into the cracks with special tools until they break up into squares about a quarter of an inch thick. The uneven edges he straightens by a batting hammer, before piercing holes to take the roofing-nails, stacking the slats in sizes, and doing them up in sets.

English slaters have found their way to many lands to teach the secrets of making a roofing slat that will stand the weather of centuries without showing signs of wear. For, from whichever centre the slate may come, there are few more beautiful or lasting forms of roofing.

CORNISH CHINA CLAY

Although the Chinese are known to have used kaolin—later known as china clay—as early as the 2nd century for making their superb pottery, porcelain, and china ware, it was not until the middle of the 18th century, when a Plymouth chemist, William Cookworthy, discovered china clay at Tregoning Hill in Cornwall, that the industry was started in England.

For centuries potters throughout the world had tried to probe the secrets of the Chinese ware, which had always been—and still is—in a class on its own. Yet it took about 15 centuries for those secrets to reach Europe. Then they came by chance through a French priest writing home and revealing, quite incidentally, all the details so long sought. To him the matter appears to have held but little interest. But the whole world, with the obvious exception of China, was delighted, and it was not long before china clay was discovered in Saxony and the famous Dresden china factory was started.

China clay is produced in many countries now, but the 80-odd clay-pits of Cornwall are generally considered the best in the world, and well over 1,000,000 tons are produced in them every year. Although the industry is one of the smallest in England in that it is almost entirely exclusive to the one county, its products are widely sought. Somewhere about three-quarters of the total output is shipped overseas every year. The demand, normally, is greater than the supply, yet the industry can never grow, for it is only in the West Country that the necessary rock is to be found.

While America is one of the principal markets, the china clay is also exported to Germany, Poland, Holland, Belgium, and the Scandinavian countries, each of which has a particular need for it. The clay is used for making high-quality china and pottery, for cosmetics, medicines, coating "art" or illustration paper, for rubber and linoleum, for paint, and so on. It has many other uses, such as for the making of lead pencils and for work in the textiles industry.

Except for a brief period during the change over from the old Cornish steam-pumps to the modern electric ones, some of the plant machinery in the pits has now been working non-stop day and night since about 1780. Throughout the night men can be seen working by specially generated electric lighting. The pits present an unusual, if not very attractive, sight. The huge white pyramids of discarded sand stand out as landmarks against the skyline for miles, yet by these pyramids, in direct contrast, are the pits (142–145), going as much as 300 feet below ground, like enormous open-air hollows. Normally this industry gives work to about 8,000 men and boys of all ages, and it is no uncommon sight to find a boy in his early teens working side by side with a man of 80 or more. It is the proud boast of the clay-worker that he starts young and never "leaves off."

The first stage, entailing blasting holes into the sides of the rock with sticks of dynamite, is possibly the most difficult. Only a man with good knowledge of both the industry and of explosives can gauge the correct amount of dynamite necessary for the best results. Too little will have an inadequate effect and cause wastage, but if too much is used the clay will fly into the air, and much of it will be lost. What is required is to loosen the rock merely so as to allow the water to percolate all round and behind it when a high-pressure hose is directed against it from a platform erected near the cavity. The strength of the water forces the clay to run down in a thick milky stream through sand into a sump at the bottom of the pit. The hose is kept constantly working, the men operating it in shifts.

From the sump the clay is pumped by suspension into tanks, where it goes through a cleansing process, the sand being removed and sent on inclined railways to the top of the pit, to be used later for the making of concrete paving-blocks. When the sand has been removed the clay—now in a semi-purified state—is drawn by electric- pumps into two large stone settling-tanks at the top of the pit for further purification. These tanks, each of which measures about 150 feet by 80 feet and is some 8 feet deep, hold as much as 1,000 tons of clay. In the first, all the lighter foreign matter is removed, while in the second the water is drained off, leaving what looks like white slush. The "slush"—in reality, the china clay—is taken on the pit railway to long narrow kilns to be dried over fires for about 48 hours (143). Here, again, skill is required, for it is necessary to maintain an even temperature if scorching is to be avoided. The finished china clay is kept in dry storage awaiting shipment abroad from the Cornish ports of Fowey, Charlestown, or Par.

FLINT-KNAPPING

And before we close let us visit the men who are carrying on the oldest craft in the world—the flint-knappers of Brandon, on the borders of Norfolk and Suffolk. There are only about half a dozen of them left now, but their ancestors have been working here without pause for thousands of years. These last survivors may well be the direct descendants of those men who fashioned tools of flint before the discovery of metals, and the implements they are using for their work to-day bear a marked resemblance to the antler picks and pebble hammers of the Stone Age. Yes, theirs *must* be the oldest of all work.

Long after flint was discarded for tool-making, the knappers remained all-important. Flints were used for the earliest form of strike-a-light, and in 1686 the knappers made locks for the British Army. Indeed, they have helped in many wars, right down to the days of Napoleon. They were busy craftsmen until just over 100 years ago. Now, this oldest of all crafts is dying out—never to be revived. The few remaining knappers spend their time making gun-flints for the natives of West Africa and the Gold Coast. There is still a demand for such flints because, I am told, the natives must needs have arms to allow them to shoot game, whereas it is not thought desirable that they should be sufficiently well equipped to chance the possibility of them shooting people as well! With less efficient arms than their rulers they are less likely to cause disturbances. It is on this flimsy basis alone that the work survives, but when the present workers finally lay down their tools the mines of Brandon are likely to join those of Devon, Wiltshire, and Sussex as mere memorials to the men who first fashioned the world.

The flint-worker's craft is carried out in five stages—digging, drying, quartering, flaking, and knapping. On Ling Heath, a wide expanse of common two miles from Brandon, the flints are dug by sinking a shaft to a depth of anything up to 60 or 70 feet. Steps are cut out in the chalk walls to allow passage up and down, and the worker brings all loose flints to the surface on his head. When he reaches a good band or seam, he puts up galleries and hacks out the flint with his pick in the same way as Neolithic man. He piles his flints round the top of the mine until he has a "jag," or cartload, ready to be transported to the knappers. When the uneven blocks of flint are well dried, the craftsman selects one and places it on his knee, and quarters it by giving a series of short sharp taps with his hammer, followed by a harder blow from the elbow, to break it into even square pieces. It looks easy, but it certainly is not. Anyone can break a flint, but not necessarily into the shape he requires.

More difficult still is the flaking, which comprises tapping away the outer white crust, known as the shives, and then breaking up the flint into regular-shaped flakes, about four inches long, and containing one flat face and one knife-sharp edge. This, too, is done by hammering, but to get the best results the flint has to be struck at just the right spot, at the correct angle, and with a force varying according to the flint. Considering the complicated nature of this stage, the speed and dexterity with which these craftsmen wield their hammers is astounding. Even so, the last stage of knapping—from which the whole industry gets its name—is even more rapid. From his flakes the craftsman makes the flints for the various weapons, ranging from the musket to the pistol. After deciding for which type each is most suitable, he takes a flake in his left hand and, holding it on an iron bar fixed to a bench, gently taps it in quick succession, this way and that, until he has a neatly shaped flint of just the right proportions to suit its particular needs. Skilled as the present workers undoubtedly are, I am told that only in the matter of flaking can they justly claim superiority over Neolithic man, whose neat arrow-heads few have ever been able to copy in recent centuries.

It is sad that the days of our oldest craft should be numbered, but, as I have stressed many times, there is no place for mere sentiment, and when the flint-knapper's work has entirely lost its usefulness, it must surely die. But let us never forget those men who did so much to build the world and who made craftsmanship possible in the first place.

INDEX

The numerals in heavy type refer to the figure numbers of the illustrations.